FairTax: The Truth

FairTax: The Truth
Answering the Critics

NEAL BOORTZ
& CONGRESSMAN JOHN LINDER
WITH ROB WOODALL

HARPER

NEW YORK • LONDON • TORONTO • SYDNEY

HarperCollins books may be purchased for educational, business, or sales promotional use. For information, please write: Special Markets Department, HarperCollins Publishers, 10 East 53rd Street, New York, NY 10022.

FIRST EDITION

Library of Congress Cataloging-in-Publication Data

Boortz, Neal.
    FairTax, the truth : answering the critics / Neal Boortz and John Linder with Rob Woodall. —1st ed.
        p. cm.
    Includes bibliographical references and index.
    ISBN 978-0-06-154046-2 (pbk.)
    1. Income tax—United States.   2. Taxation—United States.
3. Income tax—Law and legislation—United States—Popular works.   I. Linder, John.   II. Woodall, Rob.   III. Title.   IV. Title: FairTax.
    HJ4652.B652 2008
    336.2'71—dc22   2007051079

ISBN-10: 0-06-154046-3
ISBN-13: 978-0-06-154046-2

08   09   10   11   12   DIX/RRD   10   9 8 7 6 5 4 3 2 1

This book is dedicated to the millions of individuals and businessmen who labor daily trying to cope with our current punishing tax code and who long for relief. We also dedicate this book to the critics of the FairTax. Set your agendas aside, approach with an open mind, and you will become FairTax supporters. As for the thousands of people inside the D.C. Beltway who make their livings gaming the current tax code, we hope one day to force you to seek another more honest line of work.

CONTENTS

CONTENTS

PREFACE:
THE BIRTH OF
A MOVEMENT

You know how these conversations get started. You and a few friends start talking about how to make the world a better place. Most likely, something—good or bad—has happened recently to precipitate it. Maybe one of you has had a stroke of good fortune: a job, a successful new business venture, a wedding or birth in the family. Maybe one of you has witnessed a tragedy and found a new gratefulness for what you have. Maybe you've just received a big hug from your spouse and kids, and you just have that "all's right in the world" feeling you want to share. However it starts, this kind of conversation: How can we spread the feeling? How can we make things better for others, the way they've been going for us?—can last for hours.

In the case of the FairTax, the conversation has lasted twelve years . . . and it's still going.

We've all talked about taxes at one time or another, and most of us have wished or wondered about improving the mess that is our federal income tax system. Many of us have even wondered about other kinds of taxes—including consumption taxes and sales taxes. It was a group of three men in Texas in 1995 whose thoughts first led them to the idea of the FairTax. Their conversation started that same way: "What's wrong? How can we help fix it?" What made it unusual is that it was a conversation among men of means—each a fabulously successful businessman and phi-lanthropist in his own right.

The three had recently participated in a successful campaign to bring about change in Texas—an effort that saved Texans $1.5 billion in insurance premiums in its first three years alone. The conversation that day in Texas was about how their experience in Texas could help them to tackle problems nationally.

Let's think beyond Texas, they mused. What are the pressing problems that are hurting our nation as a whole? Too many regulations? Too little participation in the democratic process?

Wait—what about this terrible tax code of ours?

Each of these men had spent countless hours pondering business decisions based not on what was good or bad for their employees, customers, and shareholders, but rather on what would have the best tax implications. Now, instead, they began imagining a system in which decisions could be made based on what's best for the individual or business, rather on what would fly under our convoluted tax code.

Each knew that the tax code was crippling our economy. Now they started talking about what they could do about it.

There was just one difference between our own idle conversations and this one: These gentlemen acted on their ideas. They resolved to start with a completely blank slate and see where their effort led them.

As they started researching the subject, examining volumes of tax literature, they found an endless trail of ideas for tweaking the current code to achieve specific economic or social goals: If you want to encourage ethanol production, do this. If you want to help marriages stay together, do that. If you want to help keep manufacturing jobs in this country, try the other. All these prescriptions—many of which ran counter to one another—were predicated on changing the current federal income tax code.

As the FairTax founders looked further, however, they found another collection of articles—a smaller, but more intriguing, body of thought—by scholars and theorists who believed that the United States would be best served by broad reform and bigger ideas. It was in these articles that they first lighted on the idea of "optimum reform."

As they sifted through the information, a group of fifteen brilliant scholars and theorists rose to the top of the stack. The businessmen contacted each of these highly respected thinkers, asking if they would be willing to participate in this new "optimum reform" effort. All fifteen agreed, and after a series of meetings, eight were chosen to participate.

With their business backgrounds, the three men spearheading the fledgling effort knew the value of giving the customer what he wants and needs. So once they assembled their economic team, their next step was to find out what the customer—that is, you, the American taxpayer—wanted.

Now let's digress for a moment. The fact is, we have a very strange relationship with success in this country. Everyone wants it, but a vocal minority insists on denigrating those who have achieved it. Some call this "wealth envy."

Our experience with successful people is very different. Our experience is that those who have their economic house in order are the most willing to help others find that same success. Such was the motivation for these founders of the FairTax as they began telling their friends about their quest to develop a better tax code. It wasn't long before offers of help and funding began to come in. Of course, the founders and their friends were receiving nothing for their efforts: no salary, no expense reimbursements, no perks, no profits. On the contrary, *they all made contributions* to the effort. They all had their financial houses in order; they had lawyers and accountants to sort out their tax bills and to keep them as low as possible within the law. In fact, one of the men was both a lawyer and a CPA, who had made a living for years helping others access the benefits available to them in the tax code. Abolishing the very tax code he utilized for the benefit of his clients—as the FairTax would ultimately do—offered him no special personal benefit. These men gave of themselves and their resources simply because it was the right thing to do. (Please remember that later, when we come to the subject of charitable giving: the beneficiaries of these men's efforts are the working men and women of America . . . and their children and grand-children.)

Okay, end of digression: back to the customer and what he wants.

A man named Philip Carroll, the CEO of Shell Oil, offered to help. He put the group in touch with Shell's in-house opinion researchers and Shell's outside consultants. And so the effort began.

Of course it sounds a tad optimistic in retrospect, but the group decided that a $4.5 million budget and an eighteen-month window would allow them to (a) research what was needed, (b) take the solution to Congress, and (c) help get it passed into law. Well . . . they tried. But of course these Washington outsiders never dreamed of the buzz saw they would run into when they brought the idea of comprehensive tax reform and simplification inside the Beltway. Perhaps it was better that they didn't: if they'd known the effort would take closer to eighteen years than eighteen months, they might have thought twice about the whole idea.

But begin they did.

First they did a little national polling to find out how Americans viewed the tax system and what they wanted to change. They then asked their economists to start designing an optimum tax system around the wishes of taxpayers. They set up focus groups in four major cities, delving into the wants and needs of Americans in great detail; the results of each focus group were sent back to the economists as they refined their tax proposal.

Notice anything missing here?

That's right: politics. They were looking for solutions, not more problems.

Nope, there were no politicians here. These were private-sector economists and tax experts and private citizens. This new tax plan was developed not by politicians but by the people of this country.

It was in the very first focus group that it became apparent that the income tax was only part of the problem. This particular group was held in Chicago, and one of its attendees was a gentleman who worked days at a local manufacturing plant. He talked about the impact of the *payroll* tax—not the income tax—on his life and wages. At the end of the year, he said, he got most of his income tax money back; the payroll tax, on the other hand, was by far the largest tax he paid. It was the payroll tax that confounded his ability to save for the future. Others in the group agreed. This led to one of the major elements of the FairTax idea: We can't just fix the income tax—the payroll tax needs fixing too. For the sake of Americans working for wages—which is almost every low- and middle-income American—the payroll tax would have to be included in this overarching reform.

As the focus groups and economic research continued, it became obvious that the current income tax could never provide a workable foundation for an "optimal" solution. Citizens and experts alike perceived that a new direction was needed to accomplish all the goals that were being developed.

The one idea that addressed all their concerns was a personal consumption tax.

In another of these focus groups, as the tax reform plan began to take shape, one participant commented that she appreciated the direction in which the tax plan was going—it was a "fair tax," she said, and it should have a name to reflect that. It was in this group that the name FairTax was born.

By 1997, the FairTax had taken shape. By this time, the trio of FairTax founders had become a larger group of citizens; picking up a cue from the focus group, it took the name Americans for Fair Taxation, or AFFT. (Originally, the group called itself the AFT—until one day a "cease and desist" order arrived from the American Federation of Teachers. Apparently, America is big enough for only one AFT. Not wanting to see the dues paid by America's teachers spent on such foolishness, Americans for Fair Taxation changed the acronym to AFFT. Another silly American lawsuit avoided.)

Once the initial public opinion and economic research had been completed, it was time to see how Americans would react to it. After surveying public opinion on tax issues in fifteen media markets across the country, the AFFT ran a short advertising campaign introducing the FairTax concept and what it hoped to bring to America. Then, after the ads had made their impact, it took another poll. The results surprised even the most seasoned advertising executives: people loved the FairTax and were gravitating toward it in unheard-of numbers.

To make the FairTax a reality, though, the AFFT needed more. To take the issue to Washington, D.C., it would need people who were willing to put their name behind the plan.

In another round of advertising and polling, the AFFT learned that people were willing to act on their enthusiasm for the FairTax. Yet another round of ads and polls confirmed that they'd be willing to spread the word by sharing their passion with their friends and neighbors. With such a showing of enthusiasm buoying their efforts, the AFFT developed literature, a marketing plan, a volunteer response center, and more. It gathered more than a million signatures on FairTax petitions, launched the www.fairtax.org Web site, and began the nationwide movement that continues today.

During the years when the FairTax was being developed, Texas Congressman Bill Archer was chairman of the House Ways and Means Committee, which handles all tax legislation in the U.S. House of Representatives. Chairman Archer knew of AFFT's efforts and gave it the names of several House members who might be helpful. One of those men was John Linder (R-Ga.). Another was Collin Peterson (D-Minn.). Linder met with the group in May 1999; by July of that year, he and Peterson had introduced the FairTax Act of 1999. By the end of the year, three more Democrats and three more Republicans had signed on as cosponsors. The bipartisan FairTax reform effort was under way. Since that time, the effort has grown a bit in Congress: From those eight total sponsors in 1999 and the 106th Congress, the number of FairTax sponsors has grown to *sixty-nine* in the House and five in the Senate. By the time you read this, those numbers should have grown.

The FairTax has become a national grassroots phenomenon. And you are now a part of it.

INTRODUCTION

This book is a sequel to *The FairTax Book,* which was published in 2005. No, that doesn't mean that you have to rush out and read *The FairTax Book* before you read this. Still, we suspect that when you've finished here you'll want to go back to read the original, just to expand your understanding of the history of our income tax, the concept of embedded taxes and tax compliance costs, and the ways that our current system of raising federal revenues hamstrings American business, harasses our citizens, and assaults basic common sense.

We hope to accomplish several goals with this book. First, we wish to expand your understanding of just how the FairTax will work when it is implemented. Second, we want to arm you with the ammunition you need to respond to criticisms, both petty and substantive, of the FairTax plan. And finally, we'd like to share with you our vision for the future of our country under the FairTax.

Having spent decades talking over the merits of consumption taxation with one other, it seems like just yesterday that the Americans for Fair Taxation made the FairTax an official bill in Congress. Yet 1999 was almost a decade ago. John still remembers having to teach House staffers to describe the bill as "the FairTax," not "a fair tax"—or, much worse, "the flat tax." We've both corrected literally thousands of callers and questioners by saying "We're not promoting a national retail sales tax; we're promoting the FairTax, a personal consumption tax carefully designed to capture the benefits of a national retail sales tax while minimizing the potential shortcomings of such a plan."

From those beginnings, the FairTax movement has spread across the nation. For a number of years now, for example, it has been nearly impossible to seek election to state or federal public office in the state of Georgia without taking a stand on the FairTax. The voters have demanded it. And now, with the 2008 race for the White House already in progress, George Stephanopoulos—former top adviser to President Bill Clinton, now chief Washington correspondent for ABC News—acting as the moderator of the first national Republican presidential debate, asked the candidates about the FairTax by name, trying to pin down each candidate on exactly where he stood on the issue. Why? Because the Iowa caucus is the first official vote in the presidential primary season—and the Iowa Republican Party has endorsed the FairTax by name.

From "How do you spell it?" at the staff level to "Where do you stand on it?" at the presidential level in less than a decade. Why the success? Because both economists and the voters say that the FairTax is that important. We agree, which is why we spend so much time on the issue ourselves. This book is another installment of our passion, which we believe reflects America's passion. Love the Fair-Tax or hate it, we trust that this book will have an impact on your views.

The FairTax Book notwithstanding, we understand that the FairTax may be a new concept to you. You may have heard candidates and politicians talking about it; you may even have read a few columns or editorials on the subject and bought this book to find out more about it. Before asking you to absorb all kinds of detailed references to the "prebate" or to inclusive rather than exclusive taxes, though, we should first address a more fundamental question:

What is this FairTax thing, anyway?

Instead of trying to explain the FairTax by running line by line through its legislative language, it'll probably be easier to review it principle by principle. After all, the Fair-Tax was created as a matter of principle—as an attempt to pool the wisdom of a collection of economists, citizens, academics, and business leaders and evolve a new set of ideas for fair taxation of the American people. The activist citizens who wrote the FairTax Act captured those principles and translated them faithfully into legislative language, which is found in bills introduced in both the U.S. House of Representatives (where the FairTax is known as H.R. 25) and the U.S. Senate (where it's known as S. 1025).[1] If you

---

1. Whenever a new Congress convenes (which happens every January of odd-numbered years), every piece of legislation must be reintroduced. As a result, the number of the legislation sometimes

want to comb through the legislative language, the FairTax is only 133 double-spaced pages long—a quick read. It can be found at www.thomas.gov (named for Thomas Jefferson), the Library of Congress Web page that offers citizens access to all congressional legislation. For a nonlegislative perspective, www.fairtax.org offers a great plain-English explanation of the bill.[2] Further material can be found at www.johnlinder.com and http://boortz.com.[3]

All of these sources, however, are based on the same core principles. The words of H.R. 25 found in those 133 pages on Capitol Hill? They aren't the FairTax. That language can be changed with a stroke of a pen—and FairTax supporters are always open to new ways to perfect it. The FairTax is the collection of ideas *underlying* H.R. 25. Those principles are immutable.

And what are they?

Perhaps the best way to introduce the FairTax, and the principles behind it, is to share an open letter that was sent to the president and Congress by seventy-six economists

---

changes. In the 110th Congress (in the years 2007 and 2008), the FairTax bill has the numbers H.R. 25 in the House and S. 1025 in the Senate. However, the bill numbers were different in the 109th Congress and may be different again in the 111th Congress. Even though the bill number changes, the legislative language in the bill remains substantially the same.

2. It can be found at www.fairtax.org/PDF/PlainEnglishSummary_TheFairTaxAct2007.pdf.

3. Warning: Boortz.com may not be for the faint of heart or those who are easily offended. Log in with caution.

from across the nation—economists who, like us, have put their names and reputations behind the FairTax.

Dear Mr. President, Members of Congress, and Fellow Americans,

We, the undersigned business and university economists, welcome and applaud the ongoing initiative to reform the federal tax code. We urge the President and the Congress to work together in good faith to pass and sign into federal law H.R. 25 and S. 25, which together call for:

- Eliminating all federal income taxes for individuals and corporations
- Eliminating all federal payroll withholding taxes
- Abolishing estate and capital gains taxes and
- Repealing the 16th Amendment

We are not calling for elimination of federal taxation, which would be irresponsible and undesirable. Nor does our endorsement call for reduced federal spending. The tax reform plan we endorse is revenue neutral, collecting as much federal tax revenue as the current income tax code, including payroll withholding taxes.

We are calling for elimination of federal income taxes and federal payroll withholding taxes. We endorse replacing these costly, oppressively complex,

---

and economically inefficient taxes with a progressive national retail sales tax, such as the tax plan offered by H.R. 25 and S. 25—which is also known as the FairTax Plan. The FairTax Plan has been introduced in the 109th Congress and had 54 co-sponsors in the 108th Congress.

If passed and signed into law, the FairTax Plan would:

- Enable workers and retirees to receive 100% of their paychecks and pension benefits,
- Replace all federal income and payroll taxes with a simple, progressive, visible, efficiently collected national retail sales tax, which would be levied on the final sale of newly produced goods and services,
- Rebate to all households each month the federal sales tax they pay on basic necessities, up to an independently determined level of spending (a.k.a., the poverty level, as determined by the Department of Health and Human Services), which removes the burden of federal taxation on the poor and makes the FairTax Plan as progressive as the current tax code,
- Collect the national sales tax at the retail cash register, just as 45 states already do,
- Set a federal sales tax rate that is revenue neutral, thereby raising the same amount of tax rev-

enue as now raised by federal income taxes plus payroll withholding taxes,

- Continue Social Security and Medicare benefits as provided by law; only the means of tax collection changes,
- Eliminate all filing of individual federal tax returns,
- Eliminate the IRS and all audits of individual taxpayers; only audits of retailers would be needed, greatly reducing the cost of enforcing the federal tax code,
- Allow states the option of collecting the national retail sales tax, in return for a fee, along with their state and local sales taxes,
- Collect federal sales tax from every retail consumer in the country, whether citizen or undocumented alien, which will enlarge the federal tax base,
- Collect federal sales tax on all consumption spending on new final goods and services, whether the dollars used to finance the spending are generated legally, illegally, or in the huge "underground economy,"
- Dramatically reduce federal tax compliance costs paid by businesses, which are now embedded and hidden in retail prices, placing U.S. businesses at a disadvantage in world markets,
- Bring greater accountability and visibility to federal tax collection,

- Attract foreign equity investment to the United States, as well as encourage U.S. firms to locate new capital projects in the United States that might otherwise go abroad, and
- Not tax spending for education, since H.R. 25 and S. 25 define expenditure on education to be investment, not consumption, which will make education about half as expensive for American families as it is now.

The current U.S. income tax code is widely regarded by just about everyone as unfair, complex, wasteful, confusing, and costly. Businesses and other organizations spend more than six billion hours each year complying with the federal tax code. Estimated compliance costs conservatively top $225 billion annually—costs that are ultimately embedded in retail prices paid by consumers.

The Internal Revenue Code cannot simply be "fixed," which is amply demonstrated by more than 35 years of attempted tax code reform, each round resulting in yet more complexity and unrelenting, page-after-page, mind-numbing verbiage (now exceeding 54,000 pages containing more than 2.8 million words).

Our nation's current income tax alters business decisions in ways that limit growth in productivity. The federal income tax also alters saving and investment decisions of households, which dramatically reduces the economy's potential for growth and job creation.

Payroll withholding taxes are regressive, hitting hardest those least able to pay. Simply stated, the complexity and frequently changing rules of the federal income tax code make our country less competitive in the global economy and rob the nation of its full potential for growth and job creation.

In summary, the economic benefits of the Fair-Tax Plan are compelling. The FairTax Plan eliminates the tax bias against work, saving, and investment, which would lead to higher rates of economic growth, faster growth in productivity, more jobs, lower interest rates, and a higher standard of living for the American people.

The America proposed by the FairTax Plan would feature:

- no federal income taxes,
- no payroll taxes,
- no self-employment taxes,
- no capital gains taxes,
- no gift or estate taxes,
- no alternative minimum taxes,
- no corporate taxes,
- no payroll withholding,

- no taxes on Social Security benefits or pension benefits,
- no personal tax forms,
- no personal or business income tax record keeping, and
- no personal income tax filing whatsoever.

No Internal Revenue Service; no April 15th; all gone, forever.

We believe that many Americans will favor the FairTax Plan proposed by H.R. 25 and S. 25, although some may say, "it simply can't be done." Many said the same thing to the grassroots progressives who won women the right to vote, to those who made collective bargaining a reality for union members, and to the Freedom Riders who made civil rights a reality in America.

We urge Congress not to abandon the FairTax Plan simply because it will be difficult to face the objections of entrenched special interest groups—groups who now benefit from the complexity and tax preferences of the status quo. The comparative advantage and benefits offered by the FairTax Plan to the vast majority of Americans is simply too high a cost to pay.

Therefore, we the undersigned professional and university economists, endorse a progressive national retail sales tax plan, as provided by the Fair-

Tax Plan. We urge Congress to make H.R. 25 and S. 25 federal law, and then to work swiftly to repeal the 16th Amendment.[4]

Before we get to the meat and potatoes of the FairTax plan, let's expand on one point contained in that letter, to correct any possible misconceptions.

The letter says that the FairTax creates a "national retail sales tax, which would be levied on the final sale of newly produced goods and services." However, this does *not* mean that the prices of these retail goods and services would necessarily go up.

If the FairTax has one shortcoming, it's that it's easy to attack. Perhaps the most oft-repeated demagogic attack on the FairTax is that it "will add 23 percent to the cost of everything we buy." This, as you will learn, is false. Because the FairTax is an "embedded" sales tax—that is, it will be *included* in the price you pay, not *added to* that price—it will not increase the price of the goods or services you buy. As we'll see, the retail prices you pay today *already contain* these embedded taxes; they're merely in a different form. The FairTax merely replaces one embedded tax with another.

Here's what we've seen: As people begin absorbing these points, coming to understand the FairTax more

---

4. You can view the letter—complete with the names of the signatories—at www.fairtax.org/PDF/Open_Letter.pdf.

fully—and as they become familiar with the complaints of the critics and where their logic falls apart—they tend to be won over, and more and more of them join the hundreds of thousands of FairTax volunteers and activists.

The tide is running against the income tax. Change is inevitable. That change will come upon us either chaotically or through a well-thought-out plan that promotes freedom and economic liberty while propelling our economy and our country to new heights.

Let's begin . . .

1

THE BALL IS ROLLING

Books on taxes usually sell by the dozens."

So said a conservative iconic columnist to Congressman John Linder on the occasion of the release of *The FairTax Book*. But he didn't mean it as a critique. Rather, he made the statement in utter amazement upon learning that the book had debuted at number one on the *New York Times* best-seller list.

You think the media were surprised?

Trust us, nobody was as surprised as we were when the news came (except maybe our publishers). We can't think of a book on a subject so seemingly mundane that debuted at number one. After a few weeks at the top of the list, copies of *The FairTax Book* became scarce—but the presses were put into overdrive, and before long the book became a nationwide phenomenon.

Our experience with *The FairTax Book* was a completely unexpected and thoroughly exhilarating roller-coaster ride. We learned more than we could ever have imagined about the American public and its passion for change.

We learned, for instance, that thousands of people would be willing to drive hundreds of miles just to show their support for an idea. Not for a sports team, not for a political candidate, not for a day at Disney World or the beach . . . but for an idea.

The date was May 24, 2006. The place was Duluth, Georgia, just north of Atlanta. With the help of Neal's flagship radio station, News/Talk 750 WSB, we rented a convention center with room for 4,500 people for a FairTax rally. Sean Hannity arranged to be there, and we lined up other guests like John Stossel, Herman Cain, and Clark Howard,[1] plus a little entertainment from Atlanta's own Banks and Shane.

---

1. Just in case you don't tune in to the media much, we'll tell you who these fine gentlemen are, though the fact that they know a good thing when they see it in the FairTax might be testimony enough. Sean Hannity has spent the last decade as the host of his own FOX News show and also hosts his own ABC radio show; John Stossel is an ABC News correspondent and cohost of the *20/20* television show; Herman Cain's history includes time as the CEO of Godfather's Pizza, the chairman of the Federal Reserve Bank of

Then we sat back and fretted. Here we were, setting up a rally *in the middle of the week*. After a long day at work, wouldn't people want to be home with their families? And there were plenty of other events competing for attention—including a high school graduation taking place next door to the convention center. But it was too late to turn back now—so there we sat, hoping not to be embarrassed by a lot of empty seats.

We weren't.

Hours before the start of the rally, the local police had their hands full with traffic. When the 4,500-seat venue sold out, WSB radio announced that any FairTax supporters still en route to the event should turn around and go home—there was no more room.

Some did . . . many didn't.

They kept coming, even though they knew they couldn't get inside. While 4,500 people celebrated and enjoyed the rally inside the arena, another 5,000 sat in their cars in the convention center parking lot, listening and cheering as the rally unfolded on their car radios. Rob Woodall, Linder's chief of staff and a coconspirator on these FairTax books, was one of those turned away.

Kansas City, and a candidate for U.S. Senate in the state of Georgia; and Clark Howard is a consumer advocate, hosting his own nationally syndicated radio show and writing newspaper columns, all with the theme of "save more, spend less, and avoid ripoffs." Who better than these gentlemen to support the FairTax?

After the Atlanta rally we received literally hundreds of e-mails from people who hadn't made it inside the convention center and others who had simply turned around and headed home when they heard the radio announcements. One woman who'd come all the way from Louisiana was making her way through Atlanta traffic with her husband and two neighbors when they heard on the radio that they wouldn't be able to get into the building. They turned around and went back to Louisiana but promised to be at the next rally—and early.

Now, think about that for a moment. Four people in a car drive hundreds of miles . . . *for a tax reform rally?* Then, when they're turned away, they don't scream, shout, and spin around on their eyebrows—but instead actually write us *to apologize for not getting there earlier* and then promise to make the next rally?

Our Louisiana friends didn't have to wait long. The second FairTax rally was held two months later, on July 29, in the streets of downtown Orlando. That's right: noontime . . . in July . . . in Orlando. Hot? Let us tell you about hot. The temperature on those streets was 97 degrees when the rally began—and the crowd ran as high as 11,000 people. Despite the heat and the Florida humidity, they came—and stayed—to show their support for the FairTax.

But we learned something else at that Orlando rally: that this new FairTax movement might be in for a bit of stonewalling from the media. Aerial photographs clearly showed the size of the crowd, yet at least one local television station persisted in broadcasting the "news" that only about 2,000 people had attended. We knew how many seats there were, and it was clear from the number of filled seats and the numbers standing behind those seats and down the street that this was a five-figure crowd. Somehow those 10,000 or 11,000 really sweaty people were invisible to this TV reporter.

They were all there to try to do something about *taxes,* mind you. Not for a football game, not for a rock concert, not for the *American Idol* tryouts . . . but for a *tax rally.*

And the momentum kept building. By Tuesday, May 15, 2007, when the Republicans held one of their first presidential debates in Columbia, South Carolina, we rented an arena right next to the debate venue, brought in Sean Hannity, Herman Cain, Banks and Shane, John Stossel, and the crew from Americans for Fair Taxation, and had ourselves another rally. About 8,000 people showed up this time, and just before the debate was to start all 8,000 took to the streets to march around the presidential debate venue with FairTax signs. The media? Well, they completely ignored us; instead they led the news with the exciting story that a small band of antiwar protestors had shown up nearby.

Events like this have given us a kind of rolling education in how politics works in America. Here's a short list of what we've learned while America was learning about the FairTax:

- That the FairTax is an idea people love—and an idea the media mostly love to ignore.
- That we still have a lot to learn about the forces that oppose change—but that there's still room in the vitriolic environment of American politics to debate big ideas.
- That political insiders and K Street lobbyists—who make their livings and derive immense power from maintaining and manipulating the current tax system—are thoroughly petrified by the FairTax and will do almost anything to derail it . . . including telling lies. Not ordinary innocent little lies but the boldfaced, through-their-teeth kind.
- That many congressional and campaign staffers who advise their principals on tax issues fear the FairTax—because they fear allowing their bosses to lead.
- That opponents who want to criticize the FairTax often feel compelled to misrepresent its principles— or to lie about it outright—to give themselves something to shout about.
- That the more ordinary Americans familiarize themselves with the details of the FairTax, the more those attempts at demagoguery backfire.

Some of the attacks on the FairTax have been rather personal; naturally, partisan politics have also colored the debate. Trust us, the temptation is great to call out the critics by name. That might be personally satisfying, but it would do little to advance the cause. We might let slip an occasional name where there's some personal animus behind that person's critiques. For the most part, however, we feel confident that we can convert many of our critics with clear explanations of what the FairTax really is—and what it is not. Sometimes all it takes is a little gentle nudging.

One reason we'll try not to attack people personally is that it's not always clear where the attacks are coming from. Many of our fellow supporters have written their congressmen and senators asking whether they support the FairTax, and they've forwarded us copies of the response letters they've received. Many of these letters were written by staff members who clearly have no clue what they're talking about—or who have their own agendas they want to protect.

Imagine, then, what kind of response we'd get if we led off a section of this book with something like this:

> *Our next criticism comes from Congressman Stern-faulter of East Dakotastan. Judging from the congressman's lack of understanding of the FairTax, we must assume that if you shoved his brains into a pistachio shell they'd rattle around like a BB in a boxcar.*

Land a blow like that, of course, and we'd have to write off any hope of converting Sternfaulter—even if we proved that the FairTax could cure the common cold.[2] But don't worry: if you know anything about the personality of your talk show coauthor, you'll know he's muttering under his breath about the ignorance (feigned or otherwise) of some of these critics. Some habits are hard to break.

---

2. We're not prepared to make that claim—yet. But we're looking into it.

2

WHY NOW,
AND WHY US?

The first FairTax book came out three years ago. Why a new book now?

Two words: election year.

In the coming months, we'll be electing the next president of the United States. Changing the leader of the free world is a big step all by itself, but in America we like to do things really big. So on that same day we'll also choose 435 new members of the U.S. House of Representatives[1] (that is,

---

1. Skip this footnote if you care to, but there's an important point to be made here. Now, it may be true that many politicians like to

the entire House, for you younger readers who haven't yet taken American Government 101), 33 new members of the U.S. Senate (roughly a third of that body), 11 new state governors, and literally thousands of other state and local political leaders. That one day—November 4, 2008—will change the entire face of American political leadership. And the entire thing will happen without one gun, one tank, or one drop of blood.[2] Representative government is truly an amazing thing.

Rather than fighting it out in the streets, when it comes time to change leaders we Americans wage a battle of ideas with one another. We battle over competing visions of how we should be governed, how we should live our lives, how our children should be educated. We fight over which ideas will save more American jobs and which ideas will preserve

---

ignore our Constitution, but there are some constitutional restrictions that just won't seem to go away. One of those is that every spending bill and every tax bill *must* originate in the House of Representatives. It is interesting to note that under our original Constitution the highest office for which citizens could vote was their member of the House of Representatives. Senators were chosen by the legislatures of the several states, and the president was selected by an electoral college. Our founding fathers designed a government in which the true power rests in the House, a body the electorate can change completely every two years. It is thus quite sad that so many Americans concentrate so heavily on our quadrennial presidential beauty contest.

2. Well, perhaps this isn't entirely true. Someone could trip over a hanging chad or get food poisoning licking the stamp for his absentee ballot.

more American freedom. These are daily battles, but they culminate every four years in November.

We're writing this book now because we feel that this year the FairTax needs to be part of that battle of ideas. Sadly, truth is often a casualty of the political and ideological contests that are waged in November—just as it probably will be on the evening news tonight, on the floor of the House tomorrow, and certainly on the pages of many of America's newspapers later in the week. Whenever passion prevails over reason, truth becomes a casualty. To prevent the FairTax from becoming such a casualty, we want to put the truth about the FairTax out in black and white for all to see, providing a ready reference for both politicians and voters who are seeking answers.

As we look back on our last five years together, we're almost embarrassed to tell you how much time we've spent working on the FairTax. (Our wives could tell you, but we're not sure that they would be smiling when they did.) As we've said, the FairTax idea—as captured in the legislative-speak of H.R. 25—is only 133 pages long. So all these years later, why is it that we're still explaining that short bill?

For starters, we are a very large nation, with 300 million different interests and goals.[3] This may be a short book, but make no mistake: this is a very large topic, one that can and will impact the lives of every single person living

---

3. That is, one different goal or interest for each of us. For those of you who haven't kept track of our nation's population growth, the U.S. population is now over 300 million and rising.

within our borders and perhaps an equal number who do not. That's a challenging idea for 300 million people to absorb. Of course, there are hundreds of thousands of volunteers across the country out there every day helping explain it: we're constantly amazed at how often we hear an attack on the FairTax in the press—and then see it rebutted by a supporter who is unknown to us yet is clearly informed and knowledgeable about the bill. Between the volunteers and ourselves, literally thousands of years' worth of man-hours have been spent in support of the FairTax. But the battle continues.

The good news is that the FairTax has gained so much traction on the national stage that some very serious people have begun exploring it. Some are praising it; others are criticizing it. The uninformed attacks don't merit too much attention; if you've purchased this book, you're certainly bright enough to know when a FairTax opponent is showing signs of desperation. The simple answer for most of those critics is just to suggest that they take the time to read the FairTax bill and then reconsider their attack. It could save them some embarrassment.

But the serious critics and criticisms do deserve attention, and that's what makes this book necessary. For many of you, we hope it will serve as a how-to guide for answering the tough questions you might hear from a neighbor or coworker. Our responses might seem a bit more aggressive than you need to be, but we'll leave it to you to judge when to use honey and when to bring out the vinegar.

You may be asking yourself, "Are the 133 pages of the

FairTax bill really important enough to cause all of this fuss?"

The answer is a resounding . . . wait for it . . . *no*!

Why? Because those 133 pages are simply the best effort of legislative lawyers to capture the FairTax vision in legislative language. Changing the bill is literally as easy as Congressman Linder scratching something on the back of a napkin and giving it to the House clerk. It's a fungible document, always subject to improvement.[4]

Do you know what definitely is worth the fuss? The FairTax vision. The FairTax is a collection of fundamental economic principles—and American societal goals—that are fixed and unchanging. It's the principles and goals that we're all working toward. Whatever the language we use to express it, if at the end of the day those economic principles and societal goals are passed into law, the American people can declare victory.

What are those principles? In short words, here's what we think the American tax system should be.

---

4. You can always tell the really desperate critics—you know, the ones who have a fortune tied up in the perks of the current code and do want to lose them. They want to argue about the language of H.R. 25 rather than the principles of the FairTax. If you hate our language but love our principles, help us out and give us a suggestion to make the language better. If you hate our principles and that is why you are picking at our language, we're coming for you—because the economic future of this nation is simply too precious to let you stand in the way.

- **Simple.** Any true tax reform must result in a tax code that's easy for all Americans to understand—regardless of education, occupation, or station in life. The FairTax plan is simple. It eliminates the more than 67,000 pages of complexities in the current income tax code once and for all, replacing them with a simple uniform tax on personal consumption.

- **Fair.** Fundamental tax reform must protect the poor and treat everyone else equally. No exemptions. No exclusions. No advantages. The FairTax plan is fair. It contains a rebate of the sales tax for every household, designed to cover fully the tax consequences of spending up to the poverty line. This rebate protects low-income Americans, ensuring that every household can buy necessities tax-free. Under the FairTax, all American citizens receive equal treatment.

- **Voluntary.** Americans deserve a tax system that is not coercive or intrusive. Under the FairTax, every citizen becomes a voluntary taxpayer, paying as much as he or she chooses, when he or she chooses, and how he or she chooses to spend. The individual consumer will never have to fill out a tax form or deal with the tax man again.

- **Transparent.** The cost of government should be transparent to all Americans, with no "hidden" taxes. According to a Harvard study, the current tax component in our price system averages 22 percent.

That means that the least well off among us lose 22 percent of their purchasing power from the embedded costs of income taxes, corporate taxes, payroll taxes, and compliance costs.[5] The FairTax eliminates the hidden tax component from our price system and replaces it with a visible consumption tax. Nothing is hidden. The tax you pay is right there on your receipt. Americans deserve no less.

- **Border neutral:** Any fundamental tax reform plan must ensure that our exports aren't burdened by any tax component in the price system and that imports carry the same tax burden at retail as our domestic competition. Under the FairTax, imported goods would no longer receive preferential treatment over domestically produced goods at the checkout counter. Moreover, our exports would go abroad unburdened by any tax component in the price system.

- **Industry neutral:** Any tax reform proposal must be neutral between businesses and industries. There is no good reason that our neighbor who builds a bookstore, hires our kids, votes in our elections, and supports our community should be placed at a tax disadvantage vis-à-vis an Internet bookstore. Nor is there a good reason why service providers shouldn't

---

5. You can find the full study at http://linderfairtax.house.gov. There is a lot of good information there, but a search for "Jorgenson" will take you right to the study.

be expected to help collect taxes to fund the government just as their retailer neighbors do. The first principle of government ought to be neutrality, and a plan like the FairTax ensures industry neutrality.

- **Good for Social Security and Medicare:** To succeed politically, any fundamental reform must strengthen these two bedrock social programs. The FairTax plan would strengthen Social Security and Medicare by paying Social Security and Medicare benefits out of the general sales tax revenues. The sales tax would be collected from 300 million Americans and 50 million visitors to our shores. Revenues to Social Security and Medicare would double, as we double the size of the economy in less than fifteen years under the proposal.

It's these principles and goals we care about, far more than the 133 pages that embody it in legislation. If you want to become an expert on the 133 pages of H.R. 25, you can check out www.fairtax.org, where the language is examined line by line in plain English.[6] If you want to understand the ideas behind those pages, this is the book for you. And for our money, it's these ideas that will form the basis of a coming economic revolution in America—a revolution that may represent one of our only chances to continue our

---

6. Again, the plain-English line-by-line analysis can be found at www.fairtax.org/PDF/PlainEnglishSummary_TheFairTaxAct2007 .pdf.

nation's economic success for our children and grandchildren. The FairTax isn't just about changing the way we fund the federal government. It's about freeing Americans in a host of different ways—among them freedom from the tyranny of 67,000 pages of statutes and regulations that are understood by no one—including the very IRS officers who have the authority to enforce them.[7]

Why us?

Some critics have spent an inordinate amount of time looking for ulterior motives in those who promote the FairTax. But consider this: Two of your coauthors are in our sixties.[8] Older still are the three founders, if you will, of the FairTax movement. By the time the FairTax is implemented, it's likely that those two coauthors, and all the founders, will be retired and no longer working for wages. We'll be living off of pension plans, savings, and investments. For us, even under the current system, there'll be

7. We're not picking on IRS employees. For the most part, they are victims of the tax code just like the rest of us. We're just stating the facts. For example, in 1989, the IRS reported that 31 percent of the answers that its staff gave out over the phone to taxpayers were wrong. Fourteen years later in 2003, as the tax code grew more complex, Treasury Department investigators posing as taxpayers found that 43 percent of calls received the wrong answer—or no answer at all. Hmmm . . . you think we might have a problem?
8. Rob Woodall would be the young whippersnapper. The others don't like him all that much.

no more payroll taxes and a lot fewer income taxes. If we've been smart, we may have some capital gains taxes to pay along the way; then, of course, the government will step forward with an outstretched hand when we take that eternal celestial dirt nap. But the drudgery of record-keeping and preparing tax forms will largely be over.

So why, you may wonder, do we dedicate so much of our time and energy to the FairTax?

FROM OUR FOUNDING FATHERS

When the people find that they can vote themselves money, that will herald the end of the Republic.

—Benjamin Franklin

Let's start with our children and grandchildren. We feel we've been privileged to be born and raised in this country. What makes America great isn't its government but the dynamic of a free people, with a sense of self-reliance and personal initiative, who flourish in a system of economic liberty.

The very economic system that allowed us to work for the standard of living that we enjoy today is under assault. The parents of today's baby boomers barely worked into February of each year to satisfy their tax obligations.

Their children now work almost to May.[9] Our political class shows no inclination whatsoever to reduce our cost of government. Its members can double federal government spending in the course of a decade and then scream as if they're being tortured when someone suggests that they cut that spending back by just one percentage point. Under our present system of funding the federal government, this will never change. The current income tax system gives these politicians free rein to propose tax increases on the small percentage of people who pay the lion's share of taxes—the evil, hated, filthy rich—and to spend the largesse on vote-buying programs that ensure their positions of power.

The more the federal government collects, the more some come to rely on it and all of us are forced to focus on it. Do we dare to hope for a tomorrow where we can eliminate the inordinate amount of time we spend focusing on government at the federal level and be free to pay the attention that is needed to government at the state and local level and to elected officials closer to home?

When the authors were raised, in the 1950s and '60s, the federal government wasn't the major governmental

---

9. Our friends at the Tax Foundation call this "Tax Freedom Day," and they have tracked it all the way back to 1900. If you would like to view the full report, it is available on the Tax Foundation Web site at www.taxfoundation.org/files/sr152.pdf. Look around while you are there. The Tax Foundation produces an amazing number of interesting and useful reports about America and its taxes.

topic in the barbershop and pool hall. We talked about the school board and the city council. When we talked about the federal government, it was over issues of war and peace, and there were no acrimonious debates or marches. The debate truly did end at the water's edge. We were Americans, and when our young men and women went off to fight for freedom, wherever the fight was raging, we all agreed that our troops were on the side of the Lord. We supported them and cheered them on. When we went to church each week, we prayed for them. And when they came home—at least in small-town America—we had a parade.

As our parents were just starting to raise their families, the taxes collected for the support of the federal government were modest. Corporations collected money from you by embedding their tax burden in the price of the goods you bought and remitted it to the federal government. Back then, corporate income taxes accounted for about one third of total tax collections.[10] The direct tax burden on individuals was virtually nonexistent for house-

---

10. Corporate income taxes made up at least a quarter (often much more, but averaging a third) of the federal income tax/excise tax receipts every year from 1939 to 1968. In contrast, only in 1973 and 1976 did corporate income taxes exceed a quarter of federal income tax/excise tax receipts since that time. As you know if you have followed the FairTax, we're not big fans of these embedded corporate taxes and we're glad that they are lower today than in the 1950s and '60s. We're simply making the point that the nature of taxation—and the way in which each American experiences taxation—has changed dramatically over the last fifty years.

holds up to middle-class status and not too burdensome on the rest. The payroll tax was about $100 per year.[11]

Federal government consumption didn't exceed $100 billion until 1971; the federal government was simply not a large part of our daily lives.[12] Instead, as they should have, our lives revolved around the community, the local school, and our jobs. This was the America envisioned by our founding fathers.

In the 1960s, this began to change. No, not because of the Vietnam War, but because of President Lyndon Johnson's Great Society. Beginning in 1964, Johnson put forth his plan for health care security for the elderly (Medicare) and the poor (Medicaid). Those programs laid the groundwork for Supplemental Security Income (SSI), aid to women and infant children (WIC), Temporary Aid to Needy Families (TANF, your basic welfare), SCHIP, an expansion of the food stamp program, and more.

In his Great Society speech, Johnson told America that, as a wealthy nation, we could afford to ease the health care plight of these two categories of Americans. By 1990, he as-

---

11. In 1951, contributions to "social insurance"—the payroll tax— accounted for only 10 percent of federal receipts. By 1965, social insurance contributions comprised 19 percent of federal receipts. Since 1965, that number has doubled, and now social insurance contributions make up as much as 40 percent of all federal receipts.
12. Annual federal expenditures first topped $100 billion in 1962, though this figure includes both "the cost of government" and government transfers to individuals. By 1971, the federal government was consuming more than $100 billion a year.

sured us—citing easily quantified user statistics—Medicare would cost us only $9 billion, Medicaid only $1 billion.

Sorry, all you LBJ fans, but when it came to estimating the cost of his Great Society, Johnson blew it. Badly.

In 1990, Medicare cost us not $9 billion but $110 billion.[13] At the federal level, Medicaid cost not $1 billion but $41 billion, and the states were on the hook for tens of billions of dollars more. Look for the same thing to happen with the Medicare prescription drug plan.

The burden of funding these growing entitlements fell on a larger and larger number of citizens, and all the while the federal government was playing a larger and larger role in our daily lives. The federal food stamp program, for instance, was designed simply to get rid of some agricultural surpluses while providing the means for some poor people to buy groceries. It sounded like a simple idea. But then here came the rules—rules that were left to individual grocery stores to enforce. You could buy this, but you couldn't buy that. One food item was okay as long as it was packaged in a certain way; another was off limits because it had been cooked. These regulations spread to the farm, where suddenly farmers were being told what they could grow

---

13. In fairness to Johnson, Medicare Part A cost only $67 billion in 1990. Medicare Part B, which came along after his 1965 prediction, accounts for another $43 billion in spending. We suppose that the $9 billion promise on which Johnson sold Medicare may look slightly less flawed against a $67 billion truth than it does against a $109 billion truth.

and what they couldn't. Often farmers were paid *not* to grow crops. Wealthy lawyers in Manhattan (and elsewhere) saw the opportunities and rushed out to purchase the farms where money could be earned for not farming. What a life: sit in New York City practicing law while supplementing your income with government subsidies for not growing crops on a farm you've seen maybe once in your life.

While average Americans were being hit with a higher tax burden to support these Great Society programs, they also had the dubious pleasure of watching their neighbors load the groceries purchased with these food stamps into their brand-new cars and drive out of the grocery store parking lot. Many Americans didn't enjoy the spectacle.

Politicians quickly recognized the value in using government social programs, such as the food stamp program, to buy votes. Buying votes costs money, though, and so our tax code morphed into a complicated monstrosity as politicians found new and increasingly bizarre ways to confiscate funds from groups whose votes they didn't need in order to spend that money on groups whose votes they did need. Perhaps that explains why the vast majority of individual income taxes are now paid by a very small percentage of high achievers at the top of the income scale. Their votes weren't necessarily needed, but their money certainly was.

During this transitional process, an endless parade of organizations were formed to represent special-interest groups—from manufacturers and retailers to Realtors and local Chambers of Commerce. These organizations, usually located in Washington, D.C., spent huge sums of their clients' money lobbying politicians for various accommodations in the tax code. The special-interest groups would win, and the average taxpayer—who has no lobbying organization in Washington—would lose. Whereas years ago the corporate income tax accounted for about 30 percent of the revenue collected by the federal government, today that figure is closer to 10 percent.[14] Of course, though it's still true that every penny a corporation pays in taxes is ultimately paid by whoever purchases that corporation's goods or services or by the corporation's shareholders, there's a more important point here: for years, corporate and special-interest lobbyists have been gaming our tax code for the benefit of their clients.

In due course, people's discussions about the government moved away from the school board and the city council and began to concentrate on federal programs. These were not friendly discussions, either, but heated debates about the abuses we saw and why we were being forced to pay for them.

One particular example of abuse came to the attention of Congressman Linder's staff some time ago. The man in question was a hard worker. For six or seven days every week he worked in a small country store. In the evenings he worked as a neighborhood handyman. You'd think this man was the salt of the earth . . . until you learned about

---

14. It was 10 percent in 2000, then 8 percent in 2002 and 2003. In 2006 it was 15 percent. It is lunacy to try to base a federal budget on an income tax base that jumps around so widely.

his additional source of income. While working nearly eighty hours a week, this man had managed to qualify for disability payments from both Social Security and Medicare. When he was reported to the authorities, they responded, "We have so many of those abuses that we simply do not have the budget to look into them. We have to take the word of the doctors who made the decision."

Congressman Linder offers another example:

When my mother was in her eighties, she started getting nasty collection calls from a doctor in Minnesota. He wanted payment for parts of visits that Medicare didn't cover. Unfortunately for the doctor, my mother wasn't even in Minnesota when these visits supposedly occurred. I called the doctor's office and the doctor got on the phone and told me to mind my own business. I mentioned that (a) my mother was my business, and (b) I could make his Medicare billing practices my business as well. Within the hour he called my mother and suggested that there had been an error and she owed nothing. He also assured her that he'd be correcting his record with Medicare. I called Medicare to make certain it wouldn't pay the fraudulent bills, and they said this happens so often that there simply wasn't enough staff to follow up on the "little ones."

What do all these stories of government abuse have to do with a tax revolution? The point is, the FairTax actually gives you a way to respond to such government abuses.

With the FairTax, every dollar you spend—past the money you spend on basic necessities—is a vote. You get to vote whether to continue to fund these outrageous abuses through your spending or to withhold some of your votes by investing and saving. With each decision on where to put your money, you're effectively casting a vote for a politician who wants to help clean up the mess or one who wants to perpetuate it.

During the first years of our adult lives, most of us are focused on becoming successful—on reaching the point where our future finances are secure. Upon reaching that point, many turn their attention to the generations behind them, especially their children and grandchildren. Will they have the same opportunities we had? Will they be able to work hard, make rational decisions, and flourish? Or will the coming collapse of Social Security and our punishing tax system sabotage their efforts?

We know that the FairTax offers a constructive solution to many of the economic problems facing our country today and tomorrow. If the next generation is rewarded, rather than punished, for achievement and success; if America becomes the world's number one tax haven; if politicians lose their ability to use the tax system to punish those not likely to vote for them while rewarding those more likely—if these changes are brought about by the adoption of the FairTax, we will have left our children the greatest gift possible: an America that affords them the same opportunities we had.

From that point forward, it will be up to them.

3

ECONOMIC FORCES

W̲e're not economists, nor do we claim to be. Truth be told, one of us can't really balance his own checkbook without help from his wife.[1] But we have spent a lot of time listening to economists—and learning from them.

When we delve into the minutiae of the FairTax to learn how a certain change in the language might affect the

---

1. That would be the talk-show host. And yes, we know that balancing a checkbook is an accountant's job, not an economist's . . . but we think we've made our point anyway.

labor supply in ten years, we turn to our economist allies to clarify things that neither you nor we would otherwise know (unless you're an economist, of course). But when we look beyond the details to consider the bigger economic picture, those learned experts only confirm what we already believe—validating the core assumptions that underlie our FairTax discussions with friends, family, colleagues, and others.

It doesn't take an economist, for instance, to recognize that any savvy employer will be attracted by a chance to move his jobs to a locale where he can find cheaper labor.[2] Nor does it take an economist to tell us that China is growing, as both a producer and a consumer (and as a warrior, for that matter—but that's a different book). We know intuitively that we're saving less and that the more money we Americans have, the more we want to spend. It doesn't take a professional to tell us that technology jobs are moving to India. You don't need to consult the chairman of the economics department at Harvard to understand what we all grasp intuitively.

Here's another core assumption: You get more of the behavior you reward, and less of the behavior you punish. Taxes are punishment. When you tax something, you're going to get less of whatever it is you have taxed.

------

2. Yes, the jobs belong to the employer, not the employee. Those are not your jobs that are being shipped overseas; they belong to the entity that created them, sometimes known as "the boss." If you think the job belongs to you, try taking it somewhere else.

So think about it: Just what do we tax under our current system? Work, that's what. Hard work and productivity. The harder you work, the more you achieve. The more you achieve, the more you're taxed. To make matters worse, under our "progressive" income tax system, the harder you work, the more severe the punishment actually is! Instead of ten lashes, you get twenty—and we're going to swing harder! On what level does this make any economic sense?[3]

Let's talk about other behavior: savings, for instance. Virtually every economist and financial policy expert will tell you that it's a good thing when people save money. When money is saved, it goes into a pool, which is made available to consumers and entrepreneurs who want to buy things and start businesses. Consider this: It costs about $100,000 to create a new job in our economy. When we tax savings—something we should be rewarding—people respond by saving less, and there's less money for our economic expansion, which means less money for new jobs.

In *The FairTax Book,* we wrote extensively about a Harvard University study that showed that, on average, about 22 percent of what you pay for any consumer item or service represents the embedded costs in that item—that is, the embedded costs of our current tax system.

---

3. Well, it did make some sense to Karl Marx. In his 1848 *Communist Manifesto* he listed the establishment of a progressive income tax as one of the essentials in the formation of a Communist society. Where do you think we got the idea?

Taxes, like some other similarly offensive substances, roll downhill, and you the consumer are standing at the bottom. *Catch!*

The FairTax would eliminate the embedded costs of the American tax code—taxes on capital and labor—from the retail price, allowing corporations and businesses operating in the United States to sell their goods and services in a global marketplace with no tax component. This would immediately make America the world's premier location for job creation. From a tax perspective, our production would be absolutely unbeatable in the world marketplace. Companies would rush to our shores to build manufacturing facilities so that they too could sell in a global economy with no hidden taxes inflating their prices.

When Bill Archer (R-Tex.) was chairman of the House Ways and Means Committee, he routinely quoted an informal survey of five hundred international companies located in Europe and Japan. These companies were asked, "What would you do in your long-term planning if the United States eliminated all taxes on capital and labor and taxed only personal consumption?" Eighty percent—that's four hundred out of five hundred—said they would build their next plant in America. The remaining 20 percent—the other hundred companies—said they would relocate their business to America altogether.

Why would these companies go through the trouble of moving some or all of their business back here? Simple: because operating without any tax on capital or labor would give them a huge financial advantage.

BELIEVE IT: TAXES MOVE JOBS

"To help reduce tax load,
3M to move plants abroad."

—Headline of an article in the *Wall Street Journal,*
October 10, 2007. The article reports that 3M
will be moving "more of its operations to low-tax
jurisdictions." The move is expected to increase
the company's earnings by $150 million
to $200 million.

One more thought: Perhaps you've encountered a few of those millions of tourists who come to our country every year. Well, they don't pay income taxes—not here, anyway. Nor do they pay Social Security or Medicare taxes—not under our current tax scheme. Enact the FairTax, and all of these wonderful tourists will start funding our retirement programs with every dollar they spend. If you think that's a bad deal, we'd be fascinated to know why.

A side note: Shortly after *The FairTax Book* was published, Neal Boortz received a phone call from a Brazilian politician who wanted to fly to Atlanta for a meeting with Neal to discuss the FairTax. There was a presidential election going on in Brazil, and this person wanted to run for the office on a FairTax platform. Neal declined the meeting. Why? Because that's the last thing we need: another industrialized country enacting the FairTax before we get a chance to do so here in the United States. We need to be leading this reform movement, not playing catch-up.[4]

But luring offshore jobs back to the United States is only one of the many economic forces that are driving us toward the FairTax. Let's look at some others.

∽

Would you like a grim truth? Well, here you go: America can't survive for long under the current tax system. As much as we all might like to believe otherwise, the United States is not bulletproof.[5] There's an economic bullet aimed right at the heart of our American economy, and we must either figure out how to get out of the way or take the hit.[6]

---

4. This point about leading is a big one. The race to a 0 percent tax rate can have only one winner. If America makes it to zero first, no jobs will ever again leave for tax reasons and many new jobs will come from higher tax jurisdictions. If other nations get to zero first—and the rest of the world is certainly leading that race, since the United States has the second highest business tax rates among developed nations—they will not only keep their jobs but they will take ours too, as they are already doing. We need to make this change because it is the right thing to do economically—and we need to make it soon.

5. Many of us grew up with the reality of the Soviet Union, a reality we all thought would be a part of our lives forever. All that changed rather suddenly in 1989. How quickly could things move toward the unthinkable or worse in our country?

6. Just as we were doing our final edits on the manuscript for this book, there was an announcement that the first baby boomer had stepped forward to begin collecting Social Security benefits. You do

What would you do if you opened your morning newspaper one day and read that a team of renowned astronomers and astrophysicists had determined that a five-mile-wide asteroid was on a certain collision course with the earth? What would you do if you read that this collision would occur about thirty-two years from now—say, in April 2040? Well, if you're in your seventies or eighties, with no children or grandchildren, you might think, "Durn it! That is going to be one hell of a spectacle! Wish I was going to be around to see it!" But if you're young enough that you expect to be around in 2040—or if you have children or grandchildren you care and worry about—you might demand that your government do everything in its power to destroy or divert that asteroid, or at least begin planning right now to lessen the damage and provide for recovery efforts.

Well, here's your asteroid.

Two years ago, the U.S. Government Accountability Office (GAO) completed a survey that concluded that if we continue to tax at the current level of the economy (the average since 1970 has been at about 18 percent of our gross domestic product), and if our discretionary spending (that

---

understand, don't you, that outside of the taxes currently being paid into the system, there is no money to pay this woman and the millions of other baby boomers crowding the gates behind her? That money has been spent. All of it. All that remains are some IOUs in a file cabinet in West Virginia. Someone has to come up with the money; that someone is you!

is, spending over which politicians have full control) remains at its current percentage of the total economy, by the year 2040 the entire federal revenue stream will be insufficient to pay just the interest on the federal debt.[7]

To repeat: If things don't change drastically, thirty-two years from now our federal government will need to spend every bit of its tax revenues from every single source to pay the interest on our national debt—with no money left for any government programs. Not just *some* government programs—*any* government programs.

As your elected coauthor likes to say, this is a can we can't keep kicking down the road.[8]

Now, you might think we could handle this problem by cutting back on federal spending. Well, not so much. Theoretically we could do that, but can any of you name a year when the federal government actually spent less than the year before? It hasn't happened since Lyndon Johnson transformed our economy with his Great Society, and it's not likely to happen in the future.

Unless you love the idea of endless tax increases, the only way to dodge this bullet is to grow our economy so

---

7. Honorable David M. Walker, Comptroller General, U.S. Government Accountability Office, Testimony before the Full Committee of the House Committee on Ways and Means, March 9, 2005.
8. We have one coauthor who is elected, one who runs his mouth a great deal, and one who is smarter than the other two; hereafter they shall be referred to as the "elected," the "loud," and the "studious" coauthors.

swiftly that the increased tax revenues from the growth will buy us extra time—a *lot* of extra time—to fix the problem.

And just how can we do that? Well, every nongovernment economist who has seriously studied the FairTax says that a consumption tax like the FairTax would be better than any other tax reform proposal when it comes to promoting economic growth.[9]

Politicians who look no further than the next election would be all too happy to ignore this oncoming economic asteroid. While they worry about reelection, we need to worry about the world and the country we're going to leave for our children. Pure economic necessity has brought us to the point where we cannot wait for reform any longer. The huge economic forces driving our country to the brink of fiscal destruction are simply out of control.

The first such economic force is international competition. We're competing for jobs and wealth in a global economy—and we're doing it with a bull's-eye on our backs.

---

9. We're skeptical when someone makes a claim about "every nongovernment economist" too, but check it out for yourself. You can start with a Congressional Joint Committee on Taxation report from 1997. The joint committee invited economists of many economic stripes to model what would happen if America switched from the current code to a unified income tax or a consumption tax. Every economist who modeled reported that the consumption tax would increase long-term economic growth. Some of them hated the consumption tax for other reasons, but all agreed that it provided superior long-term economic growth. You can read the full report at www.house.gov/jct/s-21-97.pdf, but it is not exactly a page-turner.

Who has had the highest-paying jobs? We have. Who has generated the most wealth? We have. Who has the most to lose in a new global economy where everyone wants what we have? We have. As we'll discuss later, nations around the world have scrapped their antiquated tax codes (i.e., codes like ours) in favor of newer, streamlined systems that help them compete globally while ensuring that their governments collect adequate revenues. One of the benefits of these tax systems is that they're "border adjustable"—that is, goods exported overseas aren't taxed, but imported goods are. See how that works? When you ship something to another country, you lower the price by removing the taxes, hoping that the other country will buy more of it and create more jobs in your country. When you bring something *in* from the other country, in contrast, you raise the price by adding all of your taxes to it, hoping that your people will buy fewer of these imported goods and domestic goods, thus creating more jobs in your country. Seems like a clever way to keep your factories open, doesn't it?

Unfortunately, as the United States struggles to compete in the global marketplace, our tax system is preventing us from reaping these benefits—even as we're competing against other nations that do.

But we're only talking about taxes, right? How many pennies could our tax system possibly be burying in the cost of our goods and services? Well, as we described in the first FairTax book, the Harvard study established that our current price system is burdened with an average embedded tax component of 22 percent.

How does that work? Every time you buy a loaf of bread, for instance, you pay a share of the tax burden of every single person and entity that played any role in putting that bread into your plastic (or paper) bag. This includes the income and payroll taxes of every individual involved in the process, as well as the shared payroll taxes and additional income taxes of every business entity. The first tax hit involves the miner who extracted the ore from the ground that will be used to make steel for tractors and plows to grow the wheat— and the hits keep on coming, ending with the tax burdens of the grocery stores where you buy the bread and of their employees. Every person and business in this chain has costs— including tax costs—and all those costs end up in the price of the product. When all is said and done, there's really only one entity in this country that actually *pays* taxes, without passing them on. That entity is you, the final consumer.

WHO PAYS TAXES?

All taxes ultimately—the consumer pays the taxes. Nobody else pays the taxes. Corporations don't pay taxes. They collect them, but they don't pay them.

—Nobel Prize–winning economist Dr. Milton Friedman
in his comments to the President's Advisory Panel on
Federal Tax Reform, March 31, 2005

Let's do a little back-of-the-envelope math. According to the Department of Commerce and the Bureau of Economic Analysis (the folks who are paid to keep track of the U.S. economy), American consumers spent about $9.2 trillion in 2006. According to the Office of Management and Budget (the White House office that tracks government finance issues), the federal government collected $2.2 trillion in income taxes and social insurance taxes that year. Now, if the consumer pays all taxes—as we outlined above—that means that roughly 24 percent of the cost of all personal consumption went to pay the embedded cost of income and social insurance taxation. That's right: our income taxes were equal to 24 percent of all consumer spending. (For these back-of-the-envelope purposes, the difference between 22 percent and 24 percent is insignificant.)

It doesn't take a big-time education in economics to understand that when your country sells all of its goods and services into the global economy with a 22 percent tax component buried in the price, people are going to look elsewhere for those goods and services. As the economic impact of our tax structure starts to take its toll on trade, companies are going to start looking for a friendlier tax venue for their operations. If these companies figure out that they can manufacture the same product or offer the same service in some other country with a lower tax cost, guess what? They're going to pack up their jobs and move them to wherever the economic sun shines more brightly.

Simply put, when we implement the FairTax—when U.S. businesses start operating with no federal tax component on either capital or labor—companies around the world will start outsourcing their jobs to America, not the other way around. The United States will become a big-time business and jobs magnet. If you see that as a problem, you're reading the wrong book.

The second economic force that is driving us inexorably to the FairTax is the cost of complying with our current tax system. The Tax Foundation estimates that last year we spent $300 billion filling out IRS paperwork. It estimates that we'll spend $325 billion this year.[10] From many conversations with tax consultants and auditors, we estimate that Americans spend in excess of $100 billion each year just to research and calculate the tax consequence of a business decision. If we're spending between $400 billion and $500 billion each year just to comply with the code, that's not just inefficient—it's mindlessly stupid! It's like paying for a dead horse: it gets you nothing. (Well, maybe a little glue and dog food.)

When President George W. Bush came into office, he inherited an economy that was in recession. Our tax revenues were declining due to a loss of jobs and minimal corporate profits. He cut taxes in 2001 and 2003. The tax cuts amounted to $1.6 trillion over ten years. The economy came roaring back, bringing in record revenues and reducing the unemployment rolls.

Given that performance, what do you think a *$4 trillion* tax cut over the next ten years would do for economic

---

10. www.taxfoundation.org/research/show/1962.html#federal compliancecosts-20061026.

growth? That's what we'd realize by just eliminating these compliance costs.[11]

The current code will continue to extract these costs. The FairTax eliminates them! Just do the math.

The third force? The underground economy. Our present complex tax code allows—even encourages—people to go "under the radar." How bad is this problem? Well, estimates are that the underground economy—those dealing in illegal or illicit behavior such as drugs or other off-the-books labor—amounts to between $1.5 trillion and $3 trillion per year. What's more, the more complex the code becomes, the easier it is to go underground and the harder it is to get caught.

Are we suggesting that the underground economy will disappear under the FairTax? No, not at all. Some people just love to cheat. That behavior isn't going to go away overnight. One thing we are sure of, though: The people who participate in this underground economy—the people who have been hiding their ill-gotten gains from our current tax system—will most certainly have to pay their share when they take their underground dollars and spend them in the legitimate marketplace. Today a drug dealer buys a Bentley or a loaf of bread with money that hasn't been taxed. No such special treatment would be available with the FairTax: buy your car, buy your bread, pay the FairTax.

---

11. For the folks who might not be math-savvy, we would get the effect of a $4 trillion tax cut by eliminating the $400 billion in tax compliance costs each year for the next ten years.

International competition, tax compliance costs, and the underground economy: all of these forces are conspiring to make an overhaul of our tax system necessary. And there's more: as long as we have an IRS that is dedicated to the cause of tracking the source and amount of income you earn, we'll continue to drive dollars offshore and keep dollars earned overseas from coming onshore.

This is a very important economic point. In our last book we cited studies that showed that Americans and American businesses have stashed somewhere around $10 trillion in offshore financial centers. These offshore deposits have been growing by more than $800 billion per year. By the time you read this book, that number will be closing in on $12 trillion.

Let's pause a moment to think about how much $1 trillion really is. Such large-scale economic matters are often discussed in terms of trillions, but how many people really understand how much a trillion is?

Let's say you've been told you have to wait for something very special for one million seconds. How long would your wait be? A little more than eleven and a half days. But what if you had to wait for one billion seconds? Well, you'd be waiting a little longer: try almost thirty-two years.

And for one trillion seconds? We'll round it off to 31,700 years. Kind of takes your breath away, doesn't it? (Then again, it's always nice to have something to look forward to . . .)

So think about that when you realize that we have more than $12 trillion sitting in offshore accounts. They're sitting there in dollars because we have the strongest economy in the world and dollars are safe. They're sitting offshore to be secret—hidden from the prying eyes of our government through the IRS.

Don't misunderstand. Most of this money sitting offshore has been earned in a perfectly legal manner and for the most part no laws are being broken by those dollars' being deposited outside of this country. Some of it has been legally earned by American corporations in their overseas operations, and they just haven't yet decided to repatriate these funds. Why? Taxes. For some reason, these American corporations just aren't all that happy with the triple—yes, triple—taxation that would hit those dollars if they were put to work in the U.S. economy.

What do we mean, triple taxes? We'll explain.

First, of course, the profits American companies earn in foreign lands are taxed there. Then, when those dollars are brought home, they're taxed again. The third hit comes when the dollars are paid to shareholders as dividends. If you were going to get whacked in the back of the head three times, wouldn't you want to hide overseas too? You can see why sometimes leaving your money offshore for a while looks like a good idea.

By the way, it's not just the big multinational corporations that are leaving their money offshore these days. Increasing numbers of small and midsized companies are banking offshore as well. Every one of their dollars is a dollar that is not working here at home in our economy to create jobs and enrich the lives of Americans.

What would happen if we got rid of these multiple layers of corporate taxation in the United States? Well, it's not too hard to figure out. If we were to adopt the FairTax, the vast majority of that money would find its way into our markets, our banks, and our economy. Can you imagine the economic growth that would result from $12 trillion in U.S. dollars coming back home to work?

There are roughly $16 trillion in financial investments in the United States today. If just half of that $12 trillion in offshore money were invested in our markets, the increased values could have prevented the bankruptcies of Delta, United, and Northwest airlines. These corporations, after all, were forced into bankruptcy because the investments they had to fund their retirement programs had fallen in value, and when the Pension Benefit Guaranty Corporation instructed them to replenish the funds, they didn't have the cash flow to do so. Instead, they went bankrupt—and dumped the retirement plans on taxpayers. If the FairTax had been in place, their stories would have had a much happier ending.

Why shouldn't we want to bring these trillions of dollars home to our markets and banks? The benefits are clear, but the only real way to bring this money back home is to stop taxing capital and begin to tax consumption—thus making the United States the largest tax haven on Earth.

All right, we know: We're talking about big dollars here—and big benefits upon their return. So some of you are bound to be skeptical. But think about this: In a FairTax conversation with former Federal Reserve chairman Alan

Greenspan, the chairman was asked if he thought this off-shore money would in fact come back into American markets in a FairTax world. Well, he said, a small portion might remain offshore for other good business reasons—but the remainder would certainly come home.

How long would it take for that to happen? he was asked. Years? Decades?

"Months," the chairman responded.

So we're talking about international competition, tax compliance costs, the underground economy, and our dollars moving offshore.

Now let's tackle the entitlement issue that is about to bankrupt us: Social Security.

The Social Security system is a $75 trillion problem. Again, just to give you a sense of scale: Let's say you started a business on the day Jesus Christ was born. Let's say you weren't exactly a good businessman, and your business lost a million dollars every day—right through yesterday. How much longer would it take before your losses added up to $1 trillion? About 718 more years should do it, give or take a few months. And that's just *one* trillion. Multiply that by seventy-five, and you have the size of the Social Security problem. That's the amount it would take to fully fund Social Security for all current workers and retirees. To realize the magnitude of the problem we're facing, consider the fact that the total of all wealth in America is about $60 trillion. We could confiscate every item of value from every American household, including cash and investments, and apply the value to the problem—and still not have enough money to fund Social Security fully. Are you starting to appreciate the incredible mess this vote-buying entitlement program has created for our children?

In the next twenty-five years, the number of retirees in America will increase by 100 percent. The number of workers paying for them will increase by only 15 percent.

Our grandchildren will not be able to afford us.

Under the FairTax, we would move from about 160 million workers funding the system through their payroll taxes to 300 million citizens—plus about 50 million foreign visitors—funding it through their purchases. No longer would high-income earners pay Social Security and Medicare taxes on only their first $97,500 of income. Instead, they'd be taxed on 100 percent of what they spend. The FairTax would double the revenues to Social Security, Medicare, and Medicaid in less than twenty years by doubling the size of the economy.

There's something else the FairTax would accomplish. It taxes wealth instead of wages. In case you've missed it, the very wealthy in our country *don't earn wages*. Result: they don't pay payroll taxes. These people spend a lot of money on attorneys and accountants to structure their financial situation in such a way that they can live off their capital gains and dividends—which are taxed at 15 percent. We're not complaining about these low tax rates on investments, mind you. Low rates are good tax policy. In fact, the FairTax would lower that rate further—to zero. The difference is that while the people we're talking about above are not substantially involved in the tax system today, the Fair-

Tax would have them involved to the tune of 23 percent of everything that they spend.

International competition, tax compliance costs, the underground economy, our dollars running offshore to work under more favorable tax systems, and the coming collapse of Social Security and other entitlement programs: all these economic realities are driving us to the point where we will be compelled to move to a pure consumption tax such as the FairTax. It's the only way we can both expand our tax base and grow our economy as we work to solve these problems. We're either going to move to a consumption tax in an orderly and controlled manner, or we're going to let chaos reign. Let's choose order, and let's hope we don't wait too long.

4

TAXATION: THE WHO, WHAT, AND HOW

The goal of the FairTax movement is not to strangle the life out of government by depriving it of needed revenue.[1] We're realists; we know taxes are an inescapable fact of life. Some argue that federal taxes are too high, others that they're too low. The one idea nobody disputes is that, high or low, taxes are here to stay. The FairTax takes account of that.

---

1. Although when we hear about the government spending $27 million seized from hardworking Americans just to see if there happen to be any ivory-billed woodpeckers left in the wild, we're sorely tempted.

Taxes have always been a fertile field for plowing by politicians, pundits, and private citizens. As long as there have been governments, there have been taxes to pay for government and people to complain about their share of that tax load. It takes no time at all to collect quotations from people back to the Roman Empire complaining about one tax or another. In the final analysis, though, the question of tax policy has nothing to do with "if" and everything to do with "who," "what," and "how": who pays the taxes, what they pay, and how they pay them.

Somehow this has managed to escape the attention of our ever-vigilant and completely neutral mainstream media in this country, but over the last several decades, the "how" part of the tax equation has been moving steadily toward the idea of taxing consumption. Consumption taxes, in the form of the value-added tax (VAT), first became a popular idea in the 1960s. During that period, sales taxes started to appear at the national level in some foreign countries. Today, more than 130 nations utilize a VAT. According to the Organization for Economic Co-operation and Development (OECD), twenty-nine of its thirty member countries have adopted a VAT or general sales tax (GST)—not a bad scorecard for consumption taxes.

What's that thirtieth country, the holdout? The United States.

Among nations with income taxes, the trend in recent years—particularly in developing nations that are trying to increase the efficiency of their taxation and the growth of their economy—has been to abolish complex and exception-ridden income tax systems and replace them with flatter, simpler codes. The results have been astounding. It surprises many people to learn that former Soviet bloc countries are leading the way. Estonia, Latvia, and Lithuania began the trend and were quickly followed by Russia, Slovakia, Serbia, Ukraine, Romania, and Georgia. (Isn't it curious that these former Communist countries are eschewing the idea of a progressive income tax in favor of various flat tax and consumption tax alternatives? After all, the progressive income tax we currently follow was made popular by none other than Karl Marx. Just start paging through your handy copy of the *Communist Manifesto* and you'll see.[2] In Marx's list of ten necessary precursors to a Communist worker's paradise, the progressive income tax sits proudly at number two—right behind the abolition of private property.)

BELIEVE IT

In America, cutting tax rates is an ideological issue.
In the former Soviet satellites of Europe,
it is increasingly not an issue at all—so obvious
is it that it gives people better lives.

—The lead of "The World Is Flattening," *Investor's Business Daily*,
September 24, 2007

---

2. If you cannot find one, perhaps you can get one on loan from your local _ _ _ _ _ _ _ _ _ _ Party headquarters. Fill in the blanks for yourself. No, we didn't put an extra letter in there.

As nations around the world have learned the value and inherent fairness of a consumption-based tax system, they've also learned that corporate taxation (or the lack thereof) plays a huge role in economic growth. Countries around the world are now engaged in friendly combat on the field of tax competition. Ireland, in recent years, has been one of the clear winners in this battle. After Ireland reduced its top corporate tax rate from 50 percent to 12.5 percent, and took other steps to simplify its tax code, the Irish economy—led by its jobs market—promptly exploded. Other European countries took notice. In the quest for more jobs and improved economic conditions, their average corporate tax rate has fallen by a third since 1992. The United States now ranks second behind Japan for the highest corporate tax rate in the OECD.[3]

In September 2007, as we were working on this book, President Bush suggested a reduction of U.S. corporate tax rates. The Treasury Department started a discussion about reducing our corporate tax rates to attract jobs as the emerging economies have done. Perhaps the European message is getting through, because the Democrat who chairs the House Ways and Means Committee said that the idea was actually worth studying.

There are two lessons here: One, if cutting corporate tax rates leads to economic growth and new jobs, imagine

---

3. Dennis Stovall and David Centers, "The Global Downfall of Corporate Tax Rates," *Journal of American Academy of Business Summer Business Review,* Summer 2007, p. 87.

what would happen if the FairTax were enacted and corporate taxes were cut to . . . say . . . *zero.* Two, the parties can work together on this—as long as it doesn't become a mindless partisan slugfest.[4]

Europe also offers some rather stark lessons in the impact of high income taxes levied on workers. For decades in Europe, just as in the United States, more work equaled higher taxes. The taxation became so onerous that many Europeans simply refused to work more than thirty or thirty-five hours a week. The diminishing returns from higher tax rates made the extra effort not worthwhile. Many Americans just assumed that European workers were lazy—not up to the standards of our own work ethic.[5] Once their tax rates were lowered, that theory was dashed. Punish harder-working people by making them pay much higher taxes, and they'd just as soon stay home and tend their garden. Reward the extra work by allowing them to keep more of their money, and you'll start hearing that hi-ho song.[6]

Demands for, and promises of, a shorter workweek seemed to be a feature of virtually all European political

---

4. Don't give up hope on bipartisanship. It can happen. Don't believe us? Guess who led the charge for the 10 percent flat tax in Bulgaria? The Socialist Party. There is never a good Socialist around when you need one.

5. That just might include one of the coauthors—the one who runs his mouth for a living.

6. From *Snow White and the Seven Dwarfs:* "Hi-ho, hi-ho, it's off to work we go." Do we have to explain everything to you?

campaigns—until the advent of Nicolas Sarkozy. Sarkozy, the newly elected president of France, has come up with a rather interesting idea that changed this equation and, we hope, has opened some eyes. Sarkozy has proposed allowing French workers to work as many hours as they choose—but requiring them to pay income tax on only the first thirty-five hours they work. The rest would be tax-free. Can you imagine what would happen to the sacrosanct forty-hour workweek in the United States if American workers could suddenly work (and get paid for) more than those forty hours—free of any federal taxation?

Now take it a step further: imagine how eager to work and how productive American workers would be if this provision were rolled back even further—so that wages weren't taxed from the first hour on, not just the fortieth. There would be a lot of people driving home from work in the dark.

As more and more Americans get behind the FairTax, that discussion can be turned from reducing corporate taxes to eliminating them altogether.

5

THE MERITS OF THE FAIRTAX: IT'S AMAZING

As we were completing this book, our nation was going through some difficult times in terms of the economy, jobs, trust in government, immigration, and our standing internationally. Now we find ourselves in the middle of an election year in which all these issues are being hotly debated.

One of the most amazing things about the FairTax is that it confronts and addresses virtually every one of the issues above, some very comprehensively. Primary among them, of course, is the economy: the FairTax was designed to confront economic forces that have been—and continue to be—eroding the firm foundation of America's economy.

But that's just a start. As we've seen, the FairTax touches on many of the biggest debates raging in America today:

- **International competition:** How can we keep our remaining jobs in America while bringing some of the jobs that have fled our tax system back home?
- **Class warfare:** How can we fund the necessary and legitimate functions of our federal government in a fair and equitable manner while ensuring that the "other guy" is paying his fair share?
- **Big government:** How can we show the American people how much their government is actually costing them—and create the simplicity and privacy in our tax system that all Americans want and deserve?
- **Immigration:** Are immigrants stealing our jobs or working for us to make us money? How many legal immigrants do we want? How can we move from the lawless and uncontrolled situation we have now to a system where our laws are honored and immigrants actually seek to assimilate and become a part of the American family?
- **Social Security and Medicare:** How can we avoid bankrupting the current generation with higher taxes to ensure that these programs will be there for our children and grandchildren?
- **China:** Is it engaged in currency manipulation or fair trade? How can we make our economic relationship with this burgeoning economy work fairly for both parties?

Every one of these issues is currently being debated on Capitol Hill and by candidates for federal office at all levels.

The amazing thing is that a single tax bill could address so many issues—and go a long way toward solving every one of them.

Let's focus on immigration for a moment. Neal can't discuss the issue on his radio show, and John can't field a question at a town hall meeting, without passions on both sides of this issue flaring. But one thing few people expect is that the solution could possibly lie in the pages of the FairTax Act.

How would that work? Once again: If we can eliminate taxes and capital and labor, and create a border-adjustable tax system that prevents our tax costs from being shipped overseas in the price of goods and services created in the United States, our country would become an eight-hundred-pound economic gorilla. We would become unbeatable in the world marketplace. No longer would other nations, other economies, be taking business and jobs away from the U.S. economy by enacting their own valuable tax reform and simplification measures. As these nations have enjoyed steady gains, we have distracted ourselves with a cacophony of politicians, from both sides of the aisle, yammering about their favorite ideas for using our federal tax code to punish people they don't like while rewarding people and industries they do.

If we want to remain competitive in the global economy, this nonsense has to stop. The FairTax would stop it cold.

Once we enact the FairTax, companies will rush to our

shores to build manufacturing facilities so that they too can sell into a global economy with no tax component in their price. What will happen then? New jobs, that's what, and an increasing demand for new workers.

This principle has been recognized by the nation's highest economic authorities. After a meeting a few years ago to talk about the FairTax, Treasury Secretary John Snow looked over his shoulder as he left the office and said, "You've just proposed the biggest magnet for capital and jobs in history." He was right.

We have a 4.5 percent unemployment rate in the United States. For years it's been said that 5 percent unemployment in our country was essentially full employment. So where can we expect to find new workers for new factories and businesses? That's where immigration comes into the picture.

The fact is, we don't have a sufficient pool of available labor in the United States to satisfy the job growth that would result from implementation of the FairTax. As companies move operations and jobs to the United States for their economic advantage, we're going to have to move workers in to fill those jobs. We'll be forced to allow more immigration from Europe. We'll be forced to expand the H1B visas for high-tech talent. And yes, we'll have to look for more workers from Latin America.

We must acknowledge that our noncitizen population has not been met warmly by a broad spectrum of the American people. This antipathy is not based on ethnicity, and it's certainly not based on the lack of a work ethic. The

American people just don't like the idea that these illegal immigrants broke our laws to come here and continue to break our laws by staying and working here. Worse yet, we resent the fact that these illegal immigrants have become a drain on our social service systems, funded by taxpayers, and that they aren't paying their share of the taxes needed to fund the systems they're using. To top it off, we aren't all that thrilled that so many politicians refuse to address this situation, for fear of losing voter support from various minority voting blocks.

Valid points all—and all addressed by the FairTax.

You'll remember that, under the FairTax, each household receives a "prebate" at the beginning of each month. The prebate is a payment from the government equal to the amount of FairTax that the household would be expected to spend during the ensuing month on the basic necessities of life. The prebate will vary depending not on income, but on the size of the household. This prebate is designed to "untax" every household up to poverty level spending. By definition, poverty level spending is that amount of spending necessary for a given sized household to buy their essentials as determined each year by the Department of Health and Human Services (DHHS).

What does this have to do with illegal immigration? Hold on.

If you're in this country illegally—no matter how much or little you earn—*no prebate for you!*

Putting aside our justifiable anger at the arrogance of people who think they have a right to enter into and work in our country illegally—and the even more infuriating arrogance of the politicians who enable them—isn't it in America's best interest to have immigrants come to our shores, work to grow our economy, pay taxes, and seek to become Americans as Europeans and others did for two centuries? We think so. We think the prebate will give immigrants an incentive to come here legally. Those who have done so—who have gone through the necessary legal steps—tend to view illegal immigration the same way American citizens do. They feel they have a stake in their new country and are just as adamant about protecting it as we are. They buy food and cars and equipment, and they pay their fair share of taxes, just as you do. Our schools and hospitals are their schools and hospitals, and they oppose their misuse just as you do.

Legal immigrants want our borders to be protected, but they also understand why others want to join them. The happy result of the FairTax is it will help us bring in qualified new *legal* immigrants from around the world.

While we're talking about immigration, let's address foreign tourism. As America under the FairTax becomes the world's predominant tax haven for business, it will also become the world's predominant tourist destination, attracting increasing numbers of tourists from Europe, Asia, and elsewhere. So guess what will happen when those tourists spend their euros, yens, pesos, and other currencies on admissions to Walt Disney World and snow globes featuring the Empire State Building? You got it! Right there in the price of those items will be the FairTax. These tourists will take their pictures and memories home and leave behind no small amount of money to help fund the operations of our federal government—including our Social Security and Medicaid programs.

Are you taking all of that in? Makes sense, doesn't it? And all of this from a tax bill. Impressive, don't you think?

Now let's talk for a minute about transparency. By transparency, we mean the ability of average Americans to have some realistic sense of how much of the money they earn is being used to fund the operations of our federal government. As we pointed out in *The FairTax Book,* transparency certainly isn't a part of our current structure. Very few wage earners in America today actually know how much they earn. Don't believe us? Just ask your neighbors how much they earn, and they'll likely tell you what they "take home." *Take home?* What about the money you left with your employer? The income taxes, the Social Security taxes, the Medicare taxes? You earned that money too, though you're barely aware of it. That sure isn't transparency.

Transparency means knowing what you've earned—and knowing how much of what you've earned you're giving to the federal government. Transparency is seeing that entry for "FairTax" on every sales receipt you pocket whenever you buy something. Transparency means knowing how much the other guy is paying—and thus being able to judge whether or not he's paying his fair share. Transparency means knowing how much *you're* paying—and thus having better information about whether you're truly getting out of government what you're putting in.

Are there downsides to tax code transparency? Oh, yeah! You bet there are! Not for you, though. The downsides are reserved for bureaucrats trying to spend your tax dollars as they see fit. If you make your living in that big domed building at the end of the National Mall in Washington, D.C., transparency would mean not just that your constituents would have a clear understanding of what they're paying but also that they would have a keener sense of how you're spending their dollars. Under the FairTax, no longer could expenditures or vote-buying programs be funded by hidden little taxes that affect only a very few. No more could one group of voters and taxpayers be played off against another group to gain favor from one at the expense of the other. Instead, people would see clearly that their tax system is inherently fair and no longer fall victim to tax code demagoguery. Good for us—if not for the political class.

The fact that FairTax principles haven't already been passed into law is an indication of failure at every level of politics and in every party. It's also an indication of the fear most politicians feel at the thought of a tax system without all those little hiding places they love to manipulate for their own benefit. You'll probably hear this from us again, but passing the FairTax would constitute the biggest transfer of power from government to the people in the history of this republic. In case you haven't noticed it, some politicians aren't all that fond of transferring power.

But remember, they're not the ones who get to choose. It's up to us. We hire those people. It's your right to let them know that there are conditions on their continued employment—passage of the FairTax being one of them.

The issue of transparency received a rush of attention in Washington recently—not on the taxation side but on the spending side. The debate was over what's called "earmarking"—the practice of inserting specific legislative language into a bill to direct a specific amount of money to a specific project. Let's say a congressman or senator wants to build a new bridge in San Francisco. The federal government sends literally hundreds of millions of dollars to California for the state to use on general transportation projects. But that congressman or senator has no way of guaranteeing that the politicians in California will choose to fund this particular bridge project. Solution? The congressman or senator inserts a specific sentence in the bill that provides the hundreds of millions of dollars to California. The sentence might read, "$X million shall be used to repair/build a bridge at Y location in San Francisco." Sometimes funding for such earmarks comes out of the pot of money a state was going to receive anyway; sometimes it's added to a state's allocated funds.[1]

---

1. This type of spending used to be called "pork barrel spending." When that name fell into general disfavor, the name was changed to "earmarking." Now people are up to speed on earmarking, including appropriations for museums at Woodstock and bridges to nowhere in Alaska, so another name is being introduced. Ladies and gentlemen . . . say goodbye to earmarks, and hello to "congressional-directed spending." Gotta love it.

Earmarks aren't limited to transportation projects, of course. They can be used for literally anything: a new gymnasium for a high school, a new golf course for a military base, a study on the effects of tanning beds, a study on the mating habits of prairie dogs, a study on breast cancer—and the list goes on.[2]

What does this have to do with taxation? Close your eyes and ponder this example. (Well, close one eye and read with the other.) Imagine the wealthiest family you know. Now imagine the poorest. Then imagine that Congressman Snord is going to put language into the next housing bill to help these two families. For the poorest family, Congressman Snord inserts language to provide $1,500 in annual housing assistance. For the wealthiest family, Congressman Snord inserts language to provide $21,000 in annual housing assistance. Now open your eye.

Now, tell us truly: How do you feel about this earmark? You know that we, your authors, don't like to pick on the wealthy. We admire hard work and success; we value the contribution of the wealthy in building businesses to employ our neighbors and putting money in our banks for other entrepreneurs to borrow to follow their own version of the American dream. But come on—does this earmark really pass your fairness test? Putting the concept of fairness aside, this earmark doesn't pass the smell test—because

---

2. One of the loud coauthor's favorites from years ago was money spent to study the mating habits of Polish Zlotnicka pigs. We don't know how that one turned out.

the government doesn't have any business handing out housing money to people who don't need it. (Whether or not it has any business handing out money at all is a different debate for a different day.)

The amazing thing is, this little fable is actually a true story. (All right, except for "Congressman Snord.") How on earth did this happen? Well, for one reason: This wasn't a "spending" earmark hidden in a spending bill; it was a "collecting" earmark, sitting right out there in the open in a tax bill. This earmark is known as the home mortgage interest deduction.

That's right. We'll bet most of you were outraged by the real-life example above—but our instincts also tell us that most of you are somewhere between ambivalent and thrilled about the home mortgage interest deduction. Why the dichotomy? We suspect that it is because the government has become very shrewd at playing games with your money. Even though the $21,000 value of the home mortgage interest deduction comes right out of the same pot at the U.S. Treasury that writing a $21,000 government check to the family would, it feels different, doesn't it?

In one case, it means letting the wealthy family keep more of its own money when it files its taxes on April 15. In the other, it means taking $21,000 out of the U.S. Treasury and mailing it to the wealthy family—$21,000 of money that was sent in by hardworking families of all economic stripes. The former may sound fair or appropriate; the latter must sound abominable. But we promise you that they're functionally exactly the same thing. At the end of the day, in either case, the U.S. government has $21,000 less in its coffers than it otherwise would. Given its rampant spending, the government either needs to tax everyone else a bit higher to cover the $21K or needs to take out yet another IOU that will in turn be passed along to our children and grandchildren.

Do you see now why this concept is so important? For decades, Congress has disguised spending projects as tax cuts. Projects that would never survive as spending line items—such as the home mortgage interest deduction—are readily embraced when they show up in the tax code. Rather than send everyone a check, we just let them add a line on their tax form. It's much easier—so much so that these "tax expenditures" (as they are known in Washington) have grown to almost $1 trillion annually. How much is that? Let's put it this way: it's almost as much money as the government spends each year on all discretionary spending programs combined. Think about that: the government "spends" nearly as much money through special lines in the tax code as it does in all of the lines of discretionary spending in the budget combined.

Is this starting to sink in? The FairTax would prevent politicians from "spending" money by inserting special lines in income tax returns—because *there wouldn't be any income tax returns*.

Another real-life example might help:

One former chairman of the Senate Finance Committee has said he opposes the FairTax because it would make it impossible to "help our friends in the business community." Now just what did he mean by "help our friends in the business community"? The answer offers an excellent example of how tax transparency might not be a good thing for some elected officials. Here's how it might work:

You may have noticed how excited everyone is about producing ethanol from corn these days—so much so that farmers are planting corn instead of other row crops. So much corn is going to the ethanol refinery that we're seeing increases in the cost of milk, beef, chicken, and pork because the producers of these animals have to pay more for feed. Even tortillas in Mexico have tripled in cost. How is this possible? Why is it happening? Very simple: the tax code now subsidizes the production of ethanol *to the tune of 51 cents a gallon*. Add to that the tariff of 54 cents a gallon on imported ethanol, and you have a tax code that's helping corn farmers and hurting the rest of us.

This is just one more line on someone's income tax return—an earmark on the tax side of the federal ledger, not the spending side. If the ethanol subsidies were on the spending side of the ledger rather than hidden in the tax code, the ethanol headlines would read differently. You'd know these subsidies exist, because there'd be a specific appropriation to pay for them. With the FairTax you'd know exactly what you were paying the federal government and exactly how the government is spending your dollars. Good for you; bad for the politicians, who might fear that transparency would affect the way you vote.

As long as every American individual and business is required to fill out a tax form each year, distributing cash through the tax code will continue to be easy—and pervasive. But what would happen if we didn't require every individual to fill out a tax form? In fact, what if—as the FairTax does—we decreed that no individual would ever fill out a tax form again? How would that $1 trillion in additional spending be disguised then? Answer: it wouldn't be. There you go. Transparency.

As these examples demonstrate, our present tax code does far more than just raise revenue for the necessary functions of government. It's both a revenue-raising tool *and* a political tool. No country or economy is well served by a tax code that lends itself to manipulation for purely political purposes—whether that purpose be to buy votes, punish adversaries, or reward supporters. The FairTax takes those manipulative tools out of politicians' hands. That's a biggie!

But here's something even bigger: the FairTax will put the United States on a level trade playing field with China.

As a nation, we're engaged in a great debate over the billions of dollars we spend on importing goods from China. After *The FairTax Book* came out, Larry Lindsey, one of President Bush's early economic advisers, stopped by Congressman Linder's office to point out that we didn't sufficiently emphasize the positive impact this would have on America with regard to imports, particularly from China. Some economists argue that the embedded cost of taxes in the price system on exports is wrung out by the floating exchange rates of the respective currencies. But China doesn't fully "float" its currency: the yuan has largely been pegged to the dollar. The FairTax, by eliminating the embedded cost of the tax system, would eliminate the disadvantage that now plagues our locally produced products relative to Chinese imports. It would effectively be a legal, WTO-compliant tariff. The Bush administration has been urging China to float its currency for six years. What China has been unwilling to do would be accomplished through implementation of the FairTax. With the FairTax in place, we would no longer care whether or not China floats its currency—though we suspect that it would begin to do so in a FairTax world, because it would be in its own self-interest.

Finally, an even larger point . . . larger than China.

In a conversation with President Bush on the FairTax, this most important point was made. He "got it." If we were the only nation in the world with no tax component in its price system, jobs and capital would flow into our country—as you've heard both former Treasury secretary John Snow and former Federal Reserve chairman Alan Greenspan say. No one disputes that. Other nations, in order to protect their jobs at home, would have to change their tax system to a pure consumption tax, such as the FairTax. That would turn their citizens into voluntary taxpayers, taking the coercion out of their tax system and spreading freedom across the planet!

If you have a better adjective, let us know. Until then, we'll just call it *amazing*.

6

MYTHS ABOUT THE FAIRTAX: IT'S NOT A MIRACLE

Maybe we should call this the "tough love" chapter. For all that the FairTax is, there are lots of things it isn't. We need to dispel some myths, and now's as good a time as any.

First, the FairTax isn't the work of a group of tax protestors. We're not trying to eliminate taxes; we're trying to reform the way they're collected. We fully understand that taxes are a fact of life. The FairTax isn't a tax cut; it isn't a stealth plan to defund the federal government. The FairTax rate will need to be set to collect just as much revenue for the operation of the federal government as the current system is collecting today.

The FairTax doesn't attempt to reduce government spending, although government spending certainly does need to be reduced. The votes aren't there to try packing both a tax reform and a spending reform plan into one piece of legislation. Our best hope is that the transparency brought about by the FairTax would encourage citizens to become more proactive in their approach to government and what it costs. Then, and only then, will we see a reduction in government spending.

The FairTax isn't a cure-all for jobs going overseas. Though it's certainly a necessary step in the right direction, there will always be cheaper fingers somewhere out there to do much of the work that needs to be done. Companies might still seek lower-cost labor elsewhere, but economists are unanimous in their belief that the FairTax would bring far more jobs—and better-paying jobs, at that—to our shores.

The FairTax isn't pain-free. As America moves from a consumption economy to a savings economy, there will be dislocations. People like to muse about the IRS employees and tax attorneys who will be laid off. That will certainly come to pass, but there will be more. For all of those businesses or even industries that have been profitable because of their advantages in the code rather than their necessity in the marketplace, the FairTax will force important changes if they want to survive.

Government largesse is addictive. Breaking addictions can be painful though necessary.

The FairTax is simply a dollar-for-dollar replacement of our current income-based revenue system with a consumption-based revenue system. As a result, it would eliminate all the disadvantages that we as a nation have placed on ourselves through the income tax system. Future refinements, such as decreased government spending, will depend on you.

It's astonishing to us how often we hear this: "I'm not going to support the FairTax because it doesn't reduce government spending." That's true, it doesn't. We've already said this, but the thought needs amplification. There are many elected officials who might well tolerate, even support, a proposal to fundamentally change the way our federal government raises revenue—that is, as long as there's still the same amount of money in the pot as before. These politicians are addicted to spending. Tax dollars buy votes, and votes keep politicians comfortably safe in their positions of power.

While the single biggest (and most accurate) complaint against the twelve-year Republican majority was that it spent too much, it's also true that a significant number of Republicans sided with the Democrats in passing spending bills, especially for education and social programs. (Bear in mind that while Congress was run for twelve years with a Republican majority, at no time was there a *conservative* majority.)

After implementation of the FairTax, the ball will be in your court. As a voter, one of your biggest challenges will be to closely monitor congressional votes on government spending and new government programs. Here, the FairTax will help. In a FairTax economy, you'll have a very special interest in watching your congressman's or senator's votes. If he or she proposes a huge new government entitlement program that would require a tax increase, he or she would have to increase taxes across the board. Everybody would be hit. No favorites. No playing off the "poor" against the evil "rich." No hiding taxes in a corporate tax code that you'll eventually pay at the retail level anyway. Though the FairTax in itself wouldn't reduce government spending, it would sure have a chilling effect on future increases.

When you see how much the federal government takes out of each purchase, we believe you'll demand that your member of Congress vote "no" more often. (And if you're unwilling to do that, shame on you.)

But perhaps the biggest FairTax myth concerns the cost of living and the size of your take-home pay. Since we want to show you how earnest we'll be about taking on real criticisms of the FairTax, let's jump into debunking this myth with both feet.

Prices and Wages

We've often heard people ask: Since the FairTax will lead to increased competition, and thus to a decline in prices, won't the cost of living remain about the same as today—while we workers will see a 50 percent increase in take-home pay?

In *The FairTax Book* we went to some lengths to explain how the concept of embedded taxes works—that they inflate the price of all goods and services we buy in the retail marketplace—and that the FairTax would erase those taxes from the price structure, replacing them with the FairTax.

As we said, we went to some lengths. Now we're going

to go to *great* lengths. There are nuances and subtleties in this equation that need to be fully explored.

First, the part of the equation dealing with embedded taxes. As we explained in *The FairTax Book,* every single entity that has anything to do with creating, developing, producing, manufacturing, marketing, and bringing a product to the retail marketplace would have a federal tax burden to pay. That tax burden would be just one of the many costs that entity incurs in the course of business—and like other costs, such as the cost of raw materials or capital equipment, that cost would be reflected in the price charged for the work.

So far, so good. A steelmaker would incorporate its tax burden into the price structure of the steel it sells to an automaker; the automaker would then incorporate its tax burden into the cost of the automobile that shows up at your dealership. Simple enough.

Now let's introduce a new element to that equation: *you,* the worker. If you're employed, you're one of the entities we've written about. It takes more than steelmakers to build a car: it also takes the people mining the ore, the people working in the steel mill, the workers on the automobile assembly line. Every one of these people has a federal tax burden associated with their labor, and that tax burden would be incorporated into the price these people charge their employer for their labor. That tax burden, along with all of the other tax burdens we've discussed, would eventually be incorporated into the retail price of the product or service.

Perhaps you've never really thought of yourself and the

work that you do in this light. In the grand scheme of things, you're just another supplier to your employer. He needs your labor just as he needs the raw materials that go into his final product. The suppliers of those raw materials charge your employer a price that leaves them with some profit after their bills are all paid. So do you—and one of the bills you have to pay is your federal tax burden.

There's one stark difference between you and the other suppliers that do business with your employer. Most of these other businesses pay their debts to the federal government on their own. In your case, however, your employer most likely does that for you—by way of withholding. Thus the concept of "take-home pay."

FIRSTHAND KNOWLEDGE

One of the things I was involved in at the Treasury was helping to design the withholding tax. . . . And the withholding tax was essential in order to collect wartime tax rates. . . . [I]t has been a mistake in the post-war period, and we would have been better off in the post-war period if we did not have a withholding.

—Nobel Prize–winning economist Dr. Milton Friedman
in his comments to the President's Advisory Panel on
Federal Tax Reform, March 31, 2005, speaking about
the birth of withholding taxes from paychecks as
a mechanism for funding World War II

Generally speaking, the tax components associated with your labor are your federal income taxes, Social Security taxes, and Medicare taxes. All of these taxes would disappear under the FairTax, just as would the federal taxes paid by your employer. Now the other entities, as we have chosen to call them, involved in bringing your particular product to the marketplace would be expected to reduce their pricing structure by an amount equal to the taxes they no longer have to pay.

So what effect would that have on you? Let's consider a couple of scenarios.

In the first scenario you would reduce the price you charge your employer for your labor by an amount equal to the tax burden you now incur by virtue of your employment. And where would that leave you? Exactly where you are right now: your take-home pay would become your paycheck. No withholding for federal taxes, no withholding for Social Security or Medicare. Your employer would no longer have to send in those payments to the federal government on your behalf. As far as your paycheck is concerned, you'd be neither harmed nor helped by the implementation of the FairTax. Your actual paycheck for the first pay period would be equal to the last paycheck you received under the old income/payroll tax scheme. Your employer would save by reducing the cost of your employment by an amount equal to the money he would normally have withheld from your check for federal income taxes, Social Security taxes, and Medicare taxes, and he could pass that savings down the line. Eventually this would lead to a reduction in the price of whatever product or service you're involved with creating.

Now for the second scenario: Your employer decides to increase your paycheck by the amount of the so-called matching contribution to Social Security and Medicare. You also decide to keep, rather than surrender to your employer, the amount that's traditionally been deducted for federal income taxes and your half of the Social Security and Medicare taxes. Result? You would start taking home a good bit more each payday. First, there would no longer be a deduction from your paycheck for federal income taxes. Then you would receive that 7.65 percent your employer has been "contributing" to Social Security and Medicare on your behalf. Suddenly you would have a lot more money to spend. In many cases, take-home paychecks would go up by 50 percent or more. Bear in mind, though, that while your disposable income (your "take-home pay") would go up substantially, the fact that you haven't reduced the price of your labor to your employer by an amount equal to your reduced tax burden would mean that your employer wouldn't be able to pass those particular tax savings down the line. To some extent, then, the price of the product or service you're involved with creating wouldn't be reduced by the full amount of the embedded taxes. Why not? Because you would keep that money to fatten your own paycheck.

What we're saying here is that in any case where the employees are willing to allow their current tax payments to be retained by and used by their employers to lower the price of production, prices of goods and services can fall—on average—by 22 percent. Conversely, in any case where products or service prices *don't* fall by 22 percent, it would be because workers decide to convert their federal tax burden into personal income—thus experiencing a sometimes substantial increase in their take-home pay.

When we first started this FairTax journey, we felt certain that all employees would be willing to stick with the same take-home pay that they have today and allow all of today's tax payments to be removed from the price of the goods and services that they produce. Well, we've been on the road for about two years now talking to you at speeches and book signings, and we have learned a shocking truth: You want to keep your money. All of it. You worked for it, you earned it, and you want to keep it. You often don't trust your employer to do the right thing and lower the price of goods. So you'd rather take home a bigger paycheck, even if it means that the price of goods might not go down as much as they otherwise might. With your new, seemingly giant take-home paycheck, you say you'd be happy to pay whatever the new pricing level will be plus the 23 percent inclusive FairTax.

So what's going to happen here? Are people going to see a huge increase in the amount of each paycheck, or are we going to see that 22 percent reduction in the cost of goods and services?

Actually, it would most likely be a combination of the two. In some workplaces the savings would be passed down the line and the cost of the final product would be reduced accordingly. In other cases, the workers would retain their tax burden plus their share of the Social Security and Medicare taxes. Their businesses wouldn't see prices go down quite as much. In some rare cases an employer might even raise employee salaries by an amount equal to the matching Social Security and Medicare "contributions," resulting in much higher paychecks. Those employers, however, would be able to reduce their prices only by an amount equal to their corporate income tax burden, tax compliance costs, and whatever tax savings have been passed on by other suppliers.

So have we changed the equation? In the final analysis, not really. Reality warns us against promising a universal 22 percent reduction in retail prices. Remember, though, with that scenario you didn't get any increase in the pay you took home. It's become clear that we're going to see a combination of reduced prices and increased paychecks. In the final analysis, we're still dealing with the same fact: *On average,* 22 percent of the cost of every product or service you buy at the retail level represents the federal tax burden associated with bringing that product or service to the marketplace. That 22 percent would be taken out of the equation through a combination of price reductions and increases in the take-home pay of working Americans. Then the application of the 23 percent embedded FairTax would bring all of our purchasing power back to just about where we are right now. Any real increase in the price of goods and services would be offset by corresponding increases in the amount of money we take home from our jobs.

෴

But what about corporate greed? you may ask.

Many of you have expressed a concern that some busi-nesses would simply keep their prices where they are, even after implementing the FairTax—trying to reap the extra profits that would come after the embedded taxes fall away. To be honest, even your coauthor (the loud one) was wor-ried about this before the publication of our first book.

That was then; this is now. Since then, your responses have answered this concern loud and clear: no businesses would succeed in maintaining their pre-FairTax prices and simply add the savings to their bottom line. Why? Because the consumers—you and your neighbors—wouldn't let them. With hundreds of thousands of FairTax volunteers spreading the word day after day, it's increasingly unlikely that any business entity could get by—for long, anyway—with such a scheme. Any business that tried this tactic would soon see its business heading for the Dumpster. Of course, that wouldn't keep some businesses from trying to keep the money and run. The way things look, though, that might be the worst business decision they'd ever made—and their second to last, just before they start think-ing about how to liquidate and close their doors.

7

THE CRITICISMS: HOW TO JUDGE THEM

Here comes the fun part—the part where we address the more serious criticisms of the FairTax. The goal here is to give you the most honest appraisal possible of the FairTax idea. We know that if we try to make the FairTax out to be something it's not—or if we allow criticisms to go unchallenged—we'll only make it more difficult for you to support and promote this tax reform idea.

Here are the criteria we've set for our evaluations:

- We want to evaluate the FairTax as it is currently conceived, not as some people would modify it.

- We want to evaluate the FairTax in light of the words of praise it frequently receives.
- We wish to evaluate the FairTax in terms of the serious criticisms leveled against it.

With those ground rules established, we believe the results will be very interesting—with many criticisms exposed as sour milk, many praises exposed as simple fantasy, and the FairTax building blocks confirmed as the solid foundation that they are.

Let's get started.

First: Can we agree that, with very few exceptions, virtually all Americans want substantive tax reform? If you don't fall into that category, we're curious as to why you're even reading this book.

Unless, that is, you're one of those who are threatened by tax reform.[1]

When it comes to tax reform, we've had more than enough feedback from Americans to name the two goals most voters share: the tax code should be simple, and it should be fair.

Something in the fabric of American character brings us to these two elements naturally. Try asking a neighbor, coworker, or family member to describe what a tax code

---

1. We're prepared to exempt many politicians and lobbyists here. Sadly, perhaps these folks are very happy with our tax system just the way it is. After all, the current tax code, devised by politicians, is thoroughly stacked in their favor! Imagine our surprise.

should be. We think you'll find "simple" and "fair" to be the most common responses. (Plenty of people might also answer that taxes should ideally be "low." Not that we disagree, but that's a different question for a different book.)

Let's look beyond average Americans to the professionals for a moment. We choose the word "professionals" intentionally rather than the more common reference to tax "experts." In our view, no one is more "expert" on the separation of the American worker from his money than the American worker. No one is more expert on what the citizenry wants in return from the government than the citizenry. But we also wanted the opinions of tax professionals, and consult them we did.

These professionals responded by saying that we should evaluate tax reform based on the following principles/criteria: Simplicity, Fairness, Economic Growth and Efficiency, Neutrality, Transparency, Minimizing Noncompliance, Impact on Government Revenues, Certainty, and Payment Convenience.

We know what you're thinking: These criteria could have been taken from a Boortz radio show or Linder speech; after all, they seem to describe the FairTax to the letter. That's no coincidence, folks. The professionals who developed these criteria started from a blank slate, much as the creators of the FairTax did. They looked at what could be and what should be rather than simply what is or what is easy.

Who are these professionals? Answer: they belong to the AICPA, the American Institute of Certified Public Accountants. That's right: CPAs made these recommendations.[2] Though naysayers always assume that CPAs are against tax reform, we have always known that individual accountants "get it," and individually CPAs tell us that they're very supportive of the FairTax. Accountants are highly educated and trained professionals who—believe us—would rather be doing more productive things for their clients than preparing tax returns. Individual CPAs tell us that with the FairTax they could be even more successful at helping businesses and individuals plan their financial future than they have been at recording their financial past.

In the chapters that follow, we'll examine the FairTax through the lens of these principles—and then examine the critics and the criticisms of the FairTax through the same lens. As we've said, America's economic future is simply too important to have it sidetracked by naysayers. We know where we need to go. These ten principles help

---

2. Though they sound like FairTax lingo, these recommendations for reform actually come directly from AICPA's October 17, 2005, release "Understanding Tax Reform: A Guide to 21st Century Alternatives." In listing these principles, the AICPA wrote, "The AICPA recommends employing the following, widely recognized indicators of good tax policy to analyze proposed changes. These ten guiding principles are equally important, and should be considered both separately and together when evaluating the current system and reform proposals." The complete AICPA report can be found on the AICPA Web site at www.aicpa.org/download/tax/AICPA_Understanding_Tax_Reform.pdf.

point the way. As we've used these critics and criticisms to help weigh the soundness of our principles, we find we've always been led to the same powerful conclusion: you're either part of the problem or part of the solution. If criticisms pass muster with the principled lens, we'll incorporate them to make the FairTax and all other reforms better. If they don't, we'll discard them as the tripe that they are, the machinations of naysayers who would rather defend their turf than move the debate forward.

And finally, we'll acknowledge the criticisms that may meet the "ten principles" test but simply move America's economic future in a different direction from the one sought by the FairTax and its advocates. While the direction pointed by these principles is clear, there may be many ways of getting there. We welcome all comers to that race. We have no pride of authorship that requires the FairTax to be the victor. Our pride is in America, not authorship. The FairTax is merely a means of moving this great country forward and unleashing its economic potential.

8

THE CRITICS

The wonderful thing about the FairTax is that it is truly a grassroots movement. It is a topic at dinner tables and water coolers across the nation. Anyone who doubts this can simply look at the "Letters to the Editor" section of the local paper. Those who support the principles of the Fair-Tax and those who oppose them bring the debate to those pages whenever the topic of taxation arises. The depth and breadth of this grassroots debate affirm that the nation is truly ready to engage on this issue and bring it to fruition.

For better or for worse, however, much of the information generated about the FairTax—and tax reform/replacement in general—isn't generated at this grassroots level. The bulk of the information comes from organizations that are pushing their own agendas. In the pages that follow, we want to look at a few of the most notable such organizations.

Americans for Fair Taxation (or FairTax.org, as it's known on the Internet) has clearly been the driving force on the "pro-FairTax" side. But it's not the only one. The National Taxpayers Union (NTU), found on the Web at www .ntu.org, has supported the FairTax and the fundamental principles behind it since 1998. The National Small Business Association (www.nsba.biz) has been another longtime advocate. As the authors of this book, we count ourselves among the "notable organizations"[1] publishing information supportive of the principles of the FairTax.

In this section, however, we'll focus not on the supporters but on the naysayers—the people and organizations who have been attacking the FairTax since the idea first gained national prominence. Some of the naysayers you will expect; some you won't.

We're constantly being asked, "Who could possibly oppose this idea?" The easiest opponents to point to when this question arises are those with a vested interest in the current code. Though these people and organizations might pay lip service to the idea of tax reform, their top criterion for supporting a reform proposal is whether or not that proposal will harm them personally.

Certainly, every major change in the tax code helps

---

1. In all humility, of course.

some and hurts others. If a change ends a tax advantage for a special-interest group, that group will be sure to oppose it. For example, the dramatic change in the depreciation schedule for commercial property in the 1986 tax reform bill caused huge losses for investors in commercial real estate. Before that bill, investors had been able to depreciate commercial property over 19 years. The new law changed that to 31.5 years.[2] For those whose investments were predicated on the tax advantage, many simply went under.[3] Perhaps we can't fault those who made those investments for being opposed to the change, but—in the case of the FairTax—we can't let the opposition from those with advantages built into the current code derail our effort to ensure the future of the American economy.[4]

_____

2. In 1993, the depreciation time period for commercial property was lengthened yet again, to 39 years. And in the six years prior to the 1986 change, it had been changed three other times. Time and time again the president and Congress have demonstrated that there is no certainty in the tax code.

3. At the time the 1986 changes to the tax code were enacted the loud coauthor owned some apartments. Thanks to the tax advantages resulting from this investment in apartments, the rents could be kept quite low. With the changes in the tax code and the resulting extension of the depreciation period, the apartments began to lose money. They were sold and bulldozed, and today expensive condominiums sit on that plot of ground. The 1986 tax reform law thus resulted in a loss of quite a few units of housing for low-income renters.

4. A disabled man once came up to us after listening to a FairTax speech and said he lived off his disability check and thus paid no

If you're reading the footnotes, you'll note that your loud coauthor once entered into an investment that made sense only because of the tax benefits he received. This is among the poorest of reasons to invest money. Investments should be made based on growth and earnings potential, not on gaming the tax code. It would be difficult indeed to quantify the damage done to our economy due to the trillions of dollars that are invested with an eye to our tax code. With the FairTax, decisions about the tax implications of an investment would be off the table. Let investments rise and fall, succeed or fail, based on the economic merits of the investment itself, not on some advantage an investor might receive from the tax code—especially when such an advantage can be taken away by the political class in a heartbeat.

People often think that accountants as a profession are invested in the current code, but our experience is that CPAs aren't at all afraid of change. Indeed, a delegation from the national professional organization of CPAs came to visit Congressman Linder to reassure him that they're not the least bit threatened by the proposal. After one FairTax speech in Saint Louis, a listener commented that surely

---

taxes. After it was explained to him that he would receive the monthly prebate to untax him up to the poverty line, he left happily. And then he said this: "Even without the prebate, this is good for my children and grandchildren." Many of those who are advantaged by the current code and yet still support the FairTax share this gentleman's support for the greater good.

the folks at H&R Block must hate the FairTax. Before long, a senior Block executive approached and said, "Don't say that. We'll make far more money helping our clients invest their money than we make filling out their tax returns. You're about to turn us into a nation of investors, and we have the largest Rolodex in the nation." For several years now, almost half of all H&R Block revenues have come from outside its Tax Services division.

If the accountants and the tax preparers aren't invested in the current code, then who is?

Let's put all industry interest groups into one category of opposition. The National Association of Realtors, for example, has made it very clear that it will fight the FairTax until the end. This group was organized with one specific goal in mind: to protect the home mortgage interest deduction. For the NAR, preserving this deduction has become a religion. A brief look at the NAR Web site will reveal articles in which the NAR states that it has no "official" position on the FairTax. Read further, however, and you'll see some of the same spurious arguments against the FairTax that are used by other organizations that have a vested interest in maintaining something close to the status quo.

Both the elected and the loud coauthors have made plenty of speeches before organizations of real estate professionals, and without exception we've found the FairTax to be well received and enthusiastically endorsed. When the subject of the home mortgage interest deduction comes up, one simple question wraps things up quite nicely: "What value would a deduction for mortgage interest have to someone who pays no income taxes?" Put it that way, and everyone gets it. It's only the professional association that doesn't. Why? Because fighting to protect tax advantages for Realtors is their only reason for being. If they're not needed for that particular fight there in Washington,[5] what are they supposed to do all day?

Another example: Five CEOs of the nation's largest life insurance companies recently visited Congressman Linder's Washington office to express their concerns. Many life insurance policies are sold with a tax advantage. When asked whether they had a product that was valuable for the average American, they all said yes. Then why did they need a tax advantage to sell it? They were forced to admit that since Americans clearly need their product, they could surely find a way to sell based on the merits of the insurance itself—not the tax advantage. The very pleasant meeting came to an end with that realization.

We're not picking on these two groups—or any other group, for that matter. It's only human nature to want to keep what you have. We simply mention them for illustrative purposes.

A second category of opponents could be labeled the "think-tank community." Most think tanks have a specific policy agenda, and if they don't believe a particular legislative proposal will help their agenda, you can bet

---

5. The offices of the National Association of Realtors are located on New Jersey Avenue in (ahem) Washington, D.C. Can you guess why? Does the word "lobbyist" come to mind?

they'll launch broadsides against that proposal out of self-defense.

In some cases, we think these groups might be mistaken in their understanding of the FairTax. In most cases, however, we think that they understand the FairTax perfectly and that we're simply going to have to agree to disagree.

- If a group thinks the tax code should be used to do more than simply raise money for the government—we'll have to agree to disagree.
- If a group thinks that gathering personal financial information from individuals and families is a legitimate function of government—a function necessary to effectively distribute government largesse—we'll have to agree to disagree.
- If a group thinks that the tax code should be a mechanism for wealth confiscation and redistribution—obviously—we'll have to agree to disagree.

(And, by "agree to disagree," we mean that we'll keep trying to change their minds on all of these issues!)

If you have the votes to mandate that our families must provide personal financial data, we suppose you'll do it over our objections. But you don't need to complicate the tax code to do it. Whatever goals someone wants to accomplish, let's have those debates—but then let's implement the outcome on the expenditures side of the federal ledger, not on the collections side. The tax code has been needlessly complicated by social agendas for far too long. Two of the coauthors have been guilty of calling on the tax code to impose social policy. It's easy to do, and our hearts are in the right place when we do it, but that doesn't make it a good idea. We need a dramatic and permanent change, like the one the FairTax provides, to put an end to "taxation as social policy" once and for all.

Now that we've identified the critics—at least by type— let's move on to the criticisms.

9

THE BAD–AND BARELY WORTH DISMISSING

This section gives us our first real chance to judge some critics and criticisms. To do so, we'll be drawing on those tax reform guidelines the accountants suggested: Simplicity, Fairness, Economic Growth and Efficiency, Neutrality, Transparency, Minimizing Noncompliance, Impact on Government Revenues, Certainty, and Payment Convenience.

Ready? Let's start with some easy ones.

Criticism: The FairTax doesn't reduce federal spending.

We're looking at that list of tax reform principles above, and "cutting spending" doesn't seem to be anywhere. Perhaps that's because cutting spending doesn't have anything to do with good tax reform. Still, many have complained angrily that the FairTax doesn't reduce spending. Well . . . you got us there. (Then again, that's why it's called the FairTax, not the FairSpend.)

As you might imagine, this spending criticism comes predominantly from the right side of the political spectrum. We sit on that right side, and we agree that spending should be reduced. There are 435 members of the House of Representatives and 100 members of the Senate. Each one of these men and women, without exception, has an interest in one or more government spending programs. The FairTax doesn't affect any of those programs. Not one. Fair-Tax supporters have enough of a battle on their hands when they approach these elected officials with a tax reform idea. If we throw spending reform into the mix, their job will only become exponentially more difficult, if not flat out impossible. It's one thing to get a majority of these 535 politicians to agree to a fundamental change in the way government spending is funded; it's quite another to get them to agree to spending reductions for their favorite programs at the same time.

The fact of the matter is, we need the votes to pass bills—and we'd lose most Democrats and about 10 percent of the Republicans if we included spending cuts.

More important, though: Where did the political right get the idea that tax bills should contain spending provisions?

The point of the FairTax isn't to decrease spending. It's to replace a costly and complicated income tax paradigm with a simple and inexpensive sales tax paradigm. That is all. We understand that many of you are concerned about the level of government spending and that your anger intensifies at the constant stream of news reports about thousands of government earmarks created as nothing less than vote-buying programs for legislators. It's our firm conviction that the tax code transparency that will come about with the FairTax will empower and encourage you to address the issue of spending by the federal government. If the people of this country can bring the necessary pressure to bear to overhaul our tax code completely, then surely those same people can turn their attention to spending and the size of government with similar effectiveness after the FairTax is in place.

It is worth noting, though, that while the FairTax itself does not try to reduce spending, it does completely separate the tax ledger and the spend ledger for the first time in decades. If that isn't a step in the right direction, we don't know what is.

Criticism: The FairTax doesn't reduce America's tax burden.

Another criticism that tends to come from the right—and even more frequently from the tax protestor crowd. If you want to protest taxes altogether, more power to you. But wouldn't it be better if you helped us to eliminate the current punishing antigrowth tax code and replace it with the FairTax first? That way we could rescue America's economy, doing away with the IRS—and you could start protesting the FairTax instead.

Look, we understand. Tax cuts are the twin sisters of spending cuts—and we'd all just love to see elected officials address both concepts more often. But when you're trying to bring about fundamental tax reform by replacing the tax code altogether, tax cuts aren't really a part of the conversation. How taxes are collected is a completely different issue from how high those taxes should be. Consult your list of tax reform principles again: you won't find tax cuts anywhere. That's a different kettle of fish.

There is one loopy Web site out there that condemns the FairTax in favor of what it calls the "No Tax Plan." Clever—but we're trying to save a nation here, and there aren't many economists who believe that we can preserve this nation by starving it of all forms of revenue.

Would we like to reduce America's tax burden? You bet. Should we do it just for the sake of doing it, while we're still running huge debts and deficits? You see the dilemma. The question of fundamental tax code replacement is complex enough without adding new layers of conflict and controversy.

To all you tax-cut advocates out there, our message for you is simple: Even though your criticism doesn't have anything to do with serious tax reform, don't give up.

Pursue it on a separate track. Just don't let it derail our first real tax reform opportunity in decades.

Finally, there's one more criticism that's barely worth responding to, but respond we must. This particular criticism came out of the clear blue sky in the fall of 2007 and smacked us right upside the head. At first we had a good "Are you &_#*%&# serious here?" type of chuckle over it—but then we sobered up. The criticism, though absurd on the face of it, could, if unanswered, do irreparable damage to the FairTax.

This particular criticism is so off the wall and dangerous that we've decided to give it its very own chapter. Here is perhaps our best example of just how far into the ozone some people will go to derail the FairTax.

Read on—carefully.

Scientology? Oh My!

Evidently the FairTax is making some people nervous. The attacks have been steadily increasing, and there's been a striking similarity in the criticisms and fabrications being offered by columnists and pundits from coast to coast.

Every once in a while, however, an attack comes from so far out in left field that it leaves FairTax supporters scratching their heads and wondering: "Where the hell did *that* come from?"

This is precisely what happened on Sunday, August 26, 2007.

This bizarre attack against the FairTax came in the form

of a *Wall Street Journal* editorial by Bruce Bartlett. Mr. Bartlett, no doubt, has some impressive credentials when it comes to matters economic. He worked in the Treasury Department as a deputy assistant secretary for economic policy from 1988 until 1993 for President George H. W. Bush. Bartlett's admirable credentials made his attack even more difficult to understand.

The column in question was titled "Fair Tax, Flawed Tax." By midday on that particular Sunday it had generated hundreds of e-mails. When we finally cleared the sleep out of our eyes and read the column we were, to put it mildly, completely stunned. For someone with a reputation this impressive to get something so important so completely wrong was more than amazing—it was stunning.

The FairTax, Bartlett said, was "originally devised by the Church of Scientology in the early 1990s as a way to get rid of the Internal Revenue Service."

Say what?

You mean that all this time we were dealing with a bunch of couch-hopping Scientologists, and we didn't even know it?

Let's put this absurd notion to rest here and now. This assertion—that the FairTax was developed by the Church of Scientology—is flat-out false. How did he get this so wrong? Just five minutes playing with the Google search engine would have set Mr. Bartlett straight. Perhaps Bartlett was screaming toward deadline. Or maybe the Google servers were down at just the wrong moment. Clearly, though, his research was flawed. What Bartlett did was to confuse two groups with tax reform agendas with each other. The Fair-Tax may well be the best tax reform proposal out there, but it certainly isn't the *only* one. Bartlett was confusing Americans for Fair Taxation (AFFT), the prime promoters of the FairTax, with another tax reform group called Citizens for an Alternative Tax System (CATS). It's possible, of course, that Bartlett allowed someone else to do his research for him on this issue—perhaps even someone with an agenda. Perhaps he blindly accepted some information from a Washington insider, such as a K Street denizen who fears the loss of power and income should the FairTax become law.

Now, please understand, we make no personal judgment of Scientology here. But we certainly recognize that being tied to Scientology can't be called the best prescription for future success.

Just who are these CATS people? Glad you asked, because the loud coauthor happens to be quite familiar with them. The fact is, Neal Boortz's interest in replacing the income tax with a national sales tax was first piqued by CATS. Before Linbeck, McNair, and Trotter even began working on the FairTax, Boortz was interviewing CATS officials on his show and talking about the benefits of a consumption tax.[1]

As it was first proposed, the CATS idea was simple: just do away with income taxes and replace them with a 17 per-

---

1. Neal developed his instinct for discussing powerfully entertaining subjects early on.

cent sales tax. Payroll taxes would stay with you, as would many other federal tax levies.

Yes, the CATS idea is still out there. But we believe the evidence clearly shows that the FairTax is the most thorough and equitable consumption tax idea out there. Twenty-two million dollars in research and development can do that for you.

Let's get back to the history of CATS and this Scientology thing. If you research the history of CATS carefully—a good one can be found on the Internet at www.cats.org—you'll see absolutely no reference to the FairTax or its founders. Nor will you find any reference to Congressman John Linder or to H.R. 25, the FairTax Act he sponsored. There is absolutely nothing there to suggest that CATS and AFFT are related.

So where does Scientology come in?

We're going to give the Google people some more business here. If you Google "Scientology Front Groups," you get no shortage of results. Just pick one that looks good and start scrolling down. When you get to the Cs, you'll see "Citizens for an Alternative Tax System."[2] As one link notes, CATS was "set up as a 'citizens' group to abolish the IRS entirely, [and] uses the 'Church of Spiritual Technology' as one of the corporations to challenge the IRS's ruling against them."

About three weeks after Bartlett made his Scientology

_____

2. We decided to click on www.lermanet.com/cos/frontgroups
.html—and there it was!

charge in *The Wall Street Journal,* AFFT Chairman and CEO Leo Linbeck wrote a letter to FairTax volunteers and the media. That letter is worth repeating here:

Bartlett's FairTax Fiction Fails to Smear
September 14, 2007

His "natural habitat" threatened by the growing popularity of the FairTax, Bruce Bartlett rather sadly resorts to the most damning fiction he can create in order to malign this thoroughly researched proposal. Misdirection is, of course, a valuable skill for pickpockets and stage magicians but in the case of public policy, it is a coarse path that reflects poorly on the performer and ill-serves honest debate.

The FairTax was developed, independently of any other proposal, over the course of several years by noted economists after extensive market research was conducted into what the public desired in the way of a national tax system. It was originally developed and has gained popular support precisely because the current income tax system has so damaged the nation and so bedevils individual taxpayers. Its origins, therefore, can be found in the sincere desire of citizens, economists, and public policy experts to see fairness, simplicity, and transparency replace the mind-numbing complexity of the tax system which so well serves self-styled experts like Mr. Bartlett.

Although not an economist, Mr. Bartlett's impressive knowledge of 65,000 pages of tax regulations and arcane minutiae of the income tax system would—overnight—of course be rendered obsolete with the paradigm-shifting simplicity of the FairTax. At the same time, foreign manufacturers would no longer see a price advantage over the "Made in America" label; taxpayers would be freed from the embarrassing and wasted $265 billion annually it costs to merely comply with the income tax system; and American earnings, investment, and productivity would no longer be subject to Congressional power struggles, the profit motives of tax lobbyists, and yes, the intellect of individuals such as Mr. Bartlett.

A federal tax policy that serves the public interest instead of personal and political ambitions is an idea that is now powerfully resonating with the public. Distortions such as Mr. Bartlett's are increasingly being seen by the public as self-serving attempts to maintain the broken and destructive income tax system. Mr. Bartlett's statement, for example, that the FairTax prebate is based on income calculations is being met with widespread laughter from a public that understands much better than Mr. Bartlett the actual design elements of the Fair-Tax. The existence of "embedded" income taxes, the logic of applying the FairTax to government spending, the difference between "inclusive" and "exclusive" calculations of both income taxes and FairTax rates, and the more than $20 million of FairTax research are permeating the public consciousness and rendering ineffective the increasingly obvious sleights-of-hand by defenders of the tax code.

Our FairTax campaign now verges on becoming a powerful national movement because the public desperately desires a better way to collect federal taxes for the common good and recognizes the current system as both inherently flawed and then further corrupted by inside-the-Beltway machinations. It is understood by those who are joining our effort that overcoming the self-interest of the increasingly disdained Congress and the army of income tax system defenders is no small task. Distortions such as Mr. Bartlett's, however, just fuel the growing grassroots wildfire to drive public policy right over the broken income tax system and all its camp followers.

Leo Linbeck

Leo Linbeck is the chairman and CEO of Americans for Fair Taxation. He is one of the founders of FairTax.org and directs the national grassroots campaign in support of the FairTax.

The Bartlett Scientology smear drew comments from other national figures. Robert McTeer, the former president

of the Dallas Federal Reserve Bank and a Distinguished
Fellow at the National Center for Policy Analysis, wrote:

> *My guess is that few readers made it with an open mind*
> *past Mr. Bartlett attributing the FairTax's origins to the*
> *Church of Scientology. That organization may have a*
> *similar proposal or a proposal with a similar name, but*
> *I know for certain that the mainstream FairTax pro-*
> *posal found at www.fairtax.org has no connection to it.*

It was clear that Bruce Bartlett owed an apology not just
to Linbeck but to the hundreds of thousands of FairTax volunteers across America.

Yet no apology was forthcoming. Instead, Bartlett renewed his attack. Knowing the facts were against him,
Bartlett desperately tried to salvage some credibility by
looking for some tie between Scientology and the FairTax.
He finally settled on the fact that some people associated
with CATS had once had a conversation with Robert A.
Mosbacher, Jr., the son of George H. W. Bush's secretary of
commerce. The CATS representative had then been referred
to Jack Trotter, one of the three FairTax founders. Trotter
and the representative had met—but nothing had come of
the meeting.

Is this the best Bartlett could do to back up his Scientology claim? Neal Boortz met with Arnold Schwarzenegger
once, and even had him on his radio show. But that doesn't
make Neal Boortz a bodybuilder!

One wonders what Bartlett would have done if he'd

ever turned his erratic research capabilities to researching the origins of the progressive income tax—in Karl Marx's *Communist Manifesto*.

As long as we're covering Bruce Bartlett's criticisms of the FairTax, we might as well get another one out of the way.

In another astonishing falsehood, Bartlett claimed that the cost of providing the prebate to every household in America has not been factored into the FairTax rate. Here, again, Bartlett is just flat wrong. The cost of the rebate most certainly *is* included in the 23 percent rate. If the rebate had not been included, the FairTax rate could have been lowered to 20 percent. The rebate is projected to cost just over 3 percent—a factor that's most certainly included in the rate.[3]

Bartlett then goes the extra mile to prove he has no idea what he's talking about when it comes to the FairTax. He claims that since the prebate is tied to household earnings, the program would lead to the "complexity and intrusiveness of tracking every American's monthly income."

Wrong. As anyone who's read either *The FairTax Book* or H.R. 25 knows, the prebate is *not* based on income, it's based on family size. There's no need to track anyone's monthly income. The only thing the government needs is

---

3. If you would like to see the most recent rate calculations, they can be found on Dr. Larry Kotlikoff's Boston University Web page (http://people.bu.edu/kotlikoff/) in the article "Taxing Sales Under the FairTax—What Rate Works?"

a valid Social Security number and the number of people in the household.

Earlier in this book we mentioned that we weren't going to call out the FairTax critics by name. We're operating on the old adage that the best way to get rid of an enemy is to make a friend of him. We don't make friends by pointing out the names behind the intellectual dishonesty that accompanies most FairTax criticisms. But one exception—for Bruce Bartlett—hardly seems excessive.

We're not sitting around in pregnant anticipation awaiting word that Bartlett has joined our cause.

10

THE GOOD–AND WORTH ANSWERING

With all of that silliness out of the way, let's get to some of the "good" criticisms. This will be the MOAC (Mother of All Chapters) in this book—long, but we think you'll agree it's the prime cut.

In this chapter, we take a look at those criticisms we hear most often and that deserve a good explanation. These "good" criticisms come in two categories: those with a grain of truth that we can easily explain and those with a grain of truth that pale in comparison with the merits of the FairTax. Again, we're always willing to consider offers of help to improve the H.R. 25 language—but if we want to rescue the American economy, there may be some warts we'll just need to live with until we can figure out how to treat them. It's been said that nobody looks good in direct sunlight (or, for that matter, on HDTV). Nobody—and no tax reform plan—is completely without tiny flaws.

One of the most rewarding things about promoting the FairTax is working with the millions of men and women across the country who are on our team. They are the true believers who, when they hear from a friend a criticism that seems to make a lot of sense, have the instinct to find the plausible explanation and take it back to that friend. They don't turn and run from conflict. They see it through. There's no substitute for working with people with that kind of commitment. For the dedicated defenders of the FairTax, we want to put these answers in your peer education arsenal. For the undecided, we hope the answers will make your decision a bit easier. For the dyed-in-the-wool opponents—well, we may never get through to you, but we want you to have the best information anyway.

Criticism: What is the rate, anyway: 23 percent or 30 percent?

From the very beginning of our efforts to transform the way we fund our federal government—and to make our tax system simple, fair, and easy to understand—our opponents have argued that we're misleading America on the FairTax rate. If you should ever hear or read that the FairTax proponents are lying, that we're trying to put one over on you, you can bet the next sentence will go something like this: "Those FairTax frauds say the sales tax rate will be 23 percent when it's obviously going to be 30 percent."

No doubt most of these critics fully understand the game they're playing. They know that if they can convince the American people that we're not telling them the whole truth, they can effectively cripple the FairTax effort—thus preserving the status quo and in many cases their power and even their very jobs. They know that the 23 percent calculation put forth by the FairTax advocates is accurate. They also know that with a bit of a mathematical and rhetorical twist they can make this figure appear to be bogus. Most important, they know that most people won't take the time to noodle this thing out on their own. They'll listen to the FairTax opponents and say "Yeah, we're being lied to. Those people are trying to trick us."

Let's see if we can't take this demagogic weapon away from the FairTax opponents. It would certainly be better for all sides to debate the FairTax on its merits rather than wasting our time on mathematical trickery.

We'll start with the simplest mathematical equation in the entire FairTax universe. After the FairTax is implemented, if you go to the store and pay $100 for an item, $23 of the cost of that item will go to the federal government. The $23 isn't added *to* the price of the item when you get to the cashier, it's included *in* the price of that item as it sits on the display shelf. That's the FairTax. Even recognizing the deficiencies of our system of public schools, most high school graduates in this country know that $23 is 23 percent of $100.

So how do these opponents and skeptics come up with the 30 percent figure? By playing on the confusion that exists between an inclusive and an exclusive sales tax, that's how. This confusion is exacerbated by the fact that virtually every one of the forty-five states that collect a sales tax computes that sales tax on an exclusive basis. That's the difference: the FairTax is computed on an inclusive basis. It's as simple as that.

All taxes—income taxes, capital gains taxes, Social Security taxes—are either inclusive or exclusive. In other words, the taxes are either included in the dollar amount being taxed or added onto it.

Virtually all income taxes are inclusive taxes—that is, they're included in the dollar amount being taxed. If you're in a 15 percent tax bracket, you are paying $15 out of every $100 you earn in income taxes. Your Social Security and Medicare taxes are also inclusive:[1] for every dollar you earn, your employer takes 7.65 cents and sends it off, along with that "matching contribution," to Washington. Your income taxes and payroll taxes aren't added *to* what you earn, they're taken *from* what you earn.

The embedded tax that presently exists on everything

---

1. We know, the federal government refers to your Social Security tax as a "contribution." Contributions are voluntary. Try telling the IRS that you want to stop volunteering to pay your Social Security tax. Then please write to let us know how that works out for you. The FairTax will get rid of Social Security taxes anyway, so we can put this "contribution" nonsense to rest.

you purchase is also inclusive. The farmer who grows the wheat factors the taxes he has to pay into the price he charges when he sells that wheat to the processor. The processor then factors his taxes into the price when he sells to the bakery. The bakery then factors those taxes into the price charged to the grocery store, and you finally end up paying them all—including the grocery store's tax burden—when you buy a loaf of bread and take it home. All those taxes, rolling downhill, are included in the purchase price of your bread.

Some taxes are noticeably different. The prime example, as we indicated above, would be state sales taxes, and this is where the confusion arises. All but five states have state sales taxes.[2] In every one of the forty-five states with a state sales tax the tax is computed on an exclusive basis. In other words, the tax is excluded *from* the price of the item as it sits there on the shelf, and then added *to* the price of the item at the cash register.

Unlike those state sales taxes, the FairTax would be an inclusive sales tax: it would be included in the sales price that you pay when you walk up to the cashier. When you see that nifty digital camera sitting there chained to the display table at your electronics store, the FairTax would be included in the price shown on the tag.

If you're a footnote reader, you know that Oregon is one of the five states without any state sales tax. This makes

_____

2. The states of Alaska, Delaware, Montana, New Hampshire, and Oregon have no state sales tax.

Oregon a perfect place to denigrate the FairTax. A columnist for *The Oregonian,* Jeff Mapes, wrote a column with the headline "30 Percent National Sales Tax Proposed to Replace IRS."[3] If you were to read Mapes's article, you wouldn't see one single reference to the correct FairTax rate of 23 percent. Instead Mapes refers to the FairTax as "a 30 percent tax on all purchases" and suggests that sales tax–averse Oregonians wouldn't be all that thrilled with the idea. Mapes's column suggests how far and wide this "30 percent" falsehood has spread. Not once in his column does he bother to distinguish between inclusive and exclusive taxes or clarify that the FairTax is included in the price of an item or service, not added to it.

Frankly, if I were an Oregonian with no knowledge of the FairTax whatsoever, Mapes's column would have frightened me to death—and sent me marching forth to join the FairTax opponents.

At this point, you may be wondering: Why don't we give in and quote the tax as exclusive rather than inclusive? Wouldn't that defeat this particular line of criticism?

The reason is simple: because the FairTax isn't designed to replace another sales tax system. It will replace the existing income tax and payroll tax system. It will replace the embedded tax system in everything you buy. Isn't it logical, not to mention honest, to quote the FairTax on the same basis that the taxes it is designed to replace are quoted?

Let's go over this again, in case you're planning to rip

---

3. *The Oregonian,* Sunday, August 19, 2007.

these questions out and stick them in your back pocket so that you'll be ready. Here's the math.

You spend $100 for a toaster. Under the FairTax plan, when you get your sales receipt it clearly shows that $23 of your $100 goes to the government as FairTax revenue.

Of course, this is where the opponents chime in: "Hold on! You're really spending $77, and then they're adding $23 tax on top of that! That works out to 30 percent!"

Now do you see the mistake they're making? They're calculating the FairTax the same way these forty-five states calculate their sales tax, by adding the tax to the price of the item at the cash register. Are they making that mistake sincerely or dishonestly? It probably depends on the character—and math skills—of the critic. But since we're quoting the FairTax on the same basis as the income taxes the FairTax will replace, we think it's only fair—not to mention correct—for our opponents to do the same.

Let's take a look at the income tax for a moment. As we've said, the income tax is quoted by the government as an inclusive tax. The most common marginal income tax rate for an American is 25 percent. Add the payroll tax, and the average American pays 33 cents of every dollar he earns to the federal government in income and payroll taxes. That leaves 67 cents[4] to spend.

---

4. Have you noticed that they don't include that little symbol for cents on computer keyboards, the way they used to on typewriters? You know, the "c" with the slash through it? What happened to it? I want it back! It's a conspiracy!

Now consider this: What would happen if the critics quoted the federal income tax on an exclusive basis, the same way they keep trying to quote the FairTax? Your 33 percent common income and payroll tax rate would suddenly become 48 percent. (And that doesn't even include the payroll tax that your employer is paying on your behalf.) Go ahead: Get out your calculator, try to remember how percentages are calculated, and give it a go! While you're at it, give some of the higher income tax rates a shot. They look pretty ugly, don't they?

But no one ever makes that mistake. (They must know they'd never get away with it.)

All we're asking is for the FairTax opponents to be honest. Shoot straight with the American people. You know the FairTax is designed to replace the income tax. Give us a fair side-by-side comparison. Compare apples to apples. If you insist on quoting your precious income tax on an inclusive basis, then do the same for the FairTax. On the other hand, if you're going to demagogue the FairTax by throwing that 30 percent figure around, at least be honest enough to quote the income and payroll taxes on the same basis. Stop telling middle Americans that they're paying a 25 percent income tax rate and a nearly 8 percent payroll tax rate when, by your logic, they're really paying a combined 48 percent.

Jeff Mapes isn't the only fellow to make this mistake. Such venerable institutions as the Ludwig von Mises Institute, an economic think tank, have published stories citing the 30 percent argument. But we do wish that these folks would check their math before hurling their slings and arrows. It would make them look smarter—and make the FairTax look as good as it really is.

FairTax supporters are not afraid of the math. If you want to continue to quote the average marginal income and payroll tax burden as being 30 percent, then use the same inclusive basis for quoting the marginal FairTax rate. If, on the other hand, you feel better quoting the FairTax rate on an exclusive basis as 30 percent, then be honest enough to start quoting the income tax the same way. Start quoting the 15 percent income tax rate as 18 percent, the 28 percent income tax rate as 39 percent, and the 38 percent rate as 61 percent . . . and then quote the 15 percent payroll tax as another 18 percent tax on top of those other rates.

It seems to us that those who oppose the FairTax come from the same crowd that is always talking about a "level playing field." Well, if you're so eager to bring that "level playing field" into play, how about debating the FairTax on just such a playing field? It is simply disingenuous[5] to insist that the tax rates be expressed differently to make it appear that the FairTax supporters are lying, or so that it appears that the income tax rate is lower than the FairTax rate.

---

5. A nice way of saying "dishonest."

Criticism: Will a 23 percent rate really be enough to fund current spending? I've been told some important government panels say the rate will need to be much higher.

This is a great criticism—because, if it were true, we'd be right there beside you stomping our feet and holding our breath until we turn blue.

But it's not true.

To show you why, let's start by playing a little game.

The two panels whose opinions are often cited on this question are the Congressional Joint Committee on Taxation and the President's Advisory Panel on Federal Tax Reform. Let's pretend, for a moment, that they're right.

Remember, the FairTax is revenue neutral. Under the FairTax, our government would collect the same amount of tax revenue as it does today under our current individual and corporate system of income taxes. So if the crazy numbers these panels quote are true—that the FairTax would amount to a sales tax of 40, 50, or 60 percent—then it must be true that this is what our government is getting from us today!

Can this be? Is it possible that it has done such a good job of disguising and hiding those taxes that we aren't really aware they're there?

We really don't believe that those who oppose the Fair-Tax and calculate wild, high rates are lying to you (well, the loud coauthor might). Generally, we believe they're just misleading you. The only real way to calculate an appropriate tax rate is to take the total amount of money the government needs to bring in and then divide that by whatever amount will be subject to tax. At the risk of being remedial for some and overly mathematical for others, if the government needs $10 and it has $100 in individual income or consumption it can tax, it will need to impose a rate of 10/100—which is 10 percent.

Given that simplicity, how do people come up with so many crazy rates for the FairTax? The answer is that they develop different assumptions about the numerator (how much money the government needs) and the denominator (how much money—either income or spending—is available to be taxed). How can that happen? Let's look at a few examples.

When FairTax.org hires economists to help to determine the rate, it chooses a single year—such as 2009—and asks the questions "How much is the government currently predicted to raise in taxes in 2009?" and "How much are Americans predicted to spend in 2009?" The calculation gets a lot more complicated when you start talking about the prebate, business-to-business sales, protecting Social Security from inflation, and more, but at its core, those are the two questions that matter.

When the president's tax panel went to calculate rates, it asked very different questions. The tax panel asked, "How much is the government predicted to raise in income taxes alone for the next ten years, assuming (a) the AMT credit will not be renewed [though it probably will be] and (b) the president's most recent tax cuts will not expire [though the Democrats controlling Congress now tell us they certainly will]?" Plus, in one of their calculations: "How much will

Americans spend on items that are currently taxable under state sales taxes?" After doing that math, the tax panel expressed the rate not in inclusive terms—as it expressed all of the income tax rates in the report—but rather as scarier tax-exclusive calculations. In the case of the tax panel, the rates it calculated were between 64 percent and 89 percent. Scary . . . and crazy . . . and meaningless. It's worth pointing out that absolutely no one we know of, anywhere in America, has ever proposed enacting the tax that the tax panel calculated. (And we stay pretty current on this stuff.) Nevertheless, those two scary numbers—64 percent and 89 percent—are now floating around out there, waiting for FairTax opponents to trot them out at the first opportunity.

The Joint Committee on Taxation performed a similar calculation back in 2000, and it too has become legend in anti-FairTax circles.

So why is it that such well-respected groups ask different questions from those the FairTax economists ask? Simple: because they're bound by bureaucratic rules and precedents. For example, the tax panel believed that President Bush prohibited it from considering anything except the income tax—in other words, that they couldn't include payroll taxes in their reform suggestions. Well, the payroll tax, which the FairTax repeals, is the largest tax 80 percent of Americans pay. So right off the bat we know that anything the tax panel concluded about a sales tax would bear little resemblance to the actual FairTax and its impact on working Americans. They entered the tax calculation game comparing apples not to oranges but to very sour grapes.

The panel and the JCT also felt bound to make projections that covered a long time period. Now, as we all know, the government finds it impossible to predict with accuracy how much money it'll spend next month; there's no reason to believe its forecasts about the next decade. Still, that never kept an economist from trying.

But here's the important point: Remember, even under current circumstances, the predictions made by the Joint Tax Committee, the Congressional Budget Office, and the Office of Management and Budget are always different from one another—and always wrong. Now try junking the entire, long-broken tax system and replacing it with a consumption tax that's predicted to drive savings rates, investment rates, and employment rates through the roof. How accurate do you think your ten-year estimates will be?

To quote from the tax panel's report: "[T]hese estimates do not account for how those behavioral changes will affect the size of the overall economy. Instead, the Treasury Department holds constant the Administration's projections for the future size of the economy. That means, for instance, that even if a reform option caused the total size of the economy to increase due to favorable investment incentives, [these] estimates would not incorporate the corresponding increase in revenues."[6]

Er, remind me—why are we going to all of this trouble to rip the tax system out by the roots and replace it with the

---

6. The final report of the President's Advisory Panel on Federal Tax Reform, November 2005, p. 44.

FairTax? Oh, yeah . . . *to increase the total size of the economy!* The tax panel admits that failing to take this into account is a problem—but then carries on without a solution.

Whenever you see a rate quoted by FairTax proponents, it will always be a one-year rate. To make sure the FairTax gets off to the right start, we've tried—to the best of our ability—to account for every foreseeable factor that might affect year one. But we know our limitations. There's just no way to predict with accuracy, for example, the dollar value of government receipts five years from now. If the economy remains static but we decide to spend more (perish the thought), we would need to vote for a higher FairTax rate. On the other hand, as the economy heats up— as all economists predict it would under a consumption tax—the FairTax (which brings in money based on the size of the economy) might well bring in *too much* money, and we'd need to vote to lower the rate before Congress spent all of the surplus on foolishness.

Finally, there's one other variant of the "23 percent isn't enough" argument we should cover. Many of the critics who oppose the FairTax on these grounds—including some think tanks—have engaged in a little . . . editing, shall we say, to support their criticism. Their tactic is simple: They rewrite H.R. 25 to incorporate a series of exclusions for the FairTax. For instance, they claim that the FairTax bill would never be passed without exemptions for food and medicine. They then take the amount of FairTax that would be raised from the sale of these items, deduct that amount from predicted revenue collections, and recalculate what the FairTax would have to be to meet current federal revenues. Somehow these critics conveniently forget to mention that the FairTax protects every household from the impact of the tax on the basic necessities of life—such as food and medicines—through the prebate mechanism. Their phony exclusions and bogus recalculations serve as yet another way of scaring the world into believing that the actual FairTax rate would be much higher than proposed.

Criticism: If the sales tax rate goes higher than 10 percent, people just won't pay it.

For a dozen years there has been an urban myth that goes as follows: studies have shown that if the sales tax rate gets above 10 percent people just won't pay it and consumption will crash. For years we've been asking for someone to step forth with a copy of just one of these "studies." So far, we haven't seen it. We've even heard this "fact" asserted by two succeeding assistant secretaries of the Treasury for tax policy; we asked both these officials for a copy of the study—and both times we were stonewalled. Finally, we discovered that our suspicions were true: The study never existed. Imagine that.

The legend of this study is traceable to Vito Tanzi, a former International Monetary Fund adviser, who offered this opinion in a symposium in a 1995 Brookings Institution publication. In a recent conversation he expressed surprise that his "casual comment" has taken on a life of its own and is quoted widely in journals and newspapers.

The irony is that Tanzi's statement is not only groundless, it's demonstrably incorrect. After all, states routinely levy hotel and restaurant taxes approaching 20 percent. That statistic points to the far more important principle when it comes to judging willingness to spend, which is known as the wealth effect: people tend to buy more and give more when they have more money in their pockets. We saw this clearly during the dot-com boom of the late 1990s.

With the combination of higher take-home pay, lower pretax prices, and the prebate, people will have the money to pay the tax—and they'll be willing to do it. In fact, once the beneficial effects of the FairTax become obvious to all, we feel confident that the American people may come to consider it their patriotic duty to eschew avoidance schemes and play the game by the rules—something our current system certainly doesn't encourage.

Criticism: The consumption tax base is more volatile/less reliable than our current income tax base.

Two questions have been raised on this topic. First: Would we be able to maintain a broad enough consumption tax base to fund essential government services if Congress started monkeying around with exemptions and exceptions? Second: Even without such congressional tinkering, would the consumption base remain sufficient to fund government services during economic downturns?

There are several ways to take on the first question. To begin with, it would make sense to compare the breadth of the consumption base with the current income tax base. The figures will show that it should be easy to improve on the current system.

Under our current income tax system, the top 1 percent of all income earners actually earn about 19 percent of all income, while paying well over one third of all income taxes.[7] The top 5 percent of income earners claim about one third of all income, yet they pay about 57 percent of all income taxes collected by the federal government. Now for the bottom half: this group earns about 13 percent of income and pays together just over 3 percent of all income taxes. Looking at these figures, does it seem evident that we've about exhausted the income base in this country when it comes to taxation? In our political climate, few politicians would dare try to increase the share of taxes paid by those in the bottom half of income earners. Given that, how much more do they think they can burden the

---

7. Odd, isn't it, that when newspapers report on some politico telling us that the rich "need to pay their fair share," we never seem to see these statistics. If your share of the tax burden being nearly twice your share of total income isn't fair, we shudder to think what these people may have in mind for high-achieving taxpayers.

high achievers without throwing the whole system into political and economic turmoil?

Percentiles Ranked by AGI*	Share of Income (percent of total)	Share of Income Taxes Paid (percent of total)
Top 1%	19.0	36.89
Top 5%	33.5	57.13
Top 10%	44.35	68.19
Top 25%	66.13	84.86
Top 50%	86.58	96.70
Bottom 50%	13.42	3.30

*Adjusted gross income.

Source: Internal Revenue Service, 2004 Individual Tax Return Data.[8]

That's half the story: currying voters' favor by pushing taxes to fewer and fewer taxpayers. The other half involves reordering the tax burden by exempting or crediting certain purchases or behaviors. The Bureau of Economic Analysis tells us that Americans made $10.3 trillion in personal income in 2005. The IRS tells us that the total adjusted gross income on 2005 individual tax returns was only $7.2 trillion. Uh-oh: Does it look to you as though some money is missing? We've lost 30 percent of the personal income base right there! But there's more: modified taxable income

---

8. You can find this information—and other interesting facts about our current broken tax system—on the IRS Web site. The information above comes from www.irs.gov/pub/irs-soi/04in05tr.xls.

in 2005—total taxable income minus all deductions and exemptions—was only $5.1 trillion. A quick calculation will reveal that the modified taxable income in this country in 2005 came to less than half the total personal income for that year. Consider this while you sit there worrying about the erosion of the consumption tax base after enactment of the FairTax: it's clear that our income tax base has already been eroded—drastically.

It's true that the above-referenced mess of an income tax system was made dysfunctional by congressional action. For example, the last major effort to simplify the income tax system was passed in 1986; succeeding Congresses have amended it *sixteen thousand times* in the last twenty years. But it's equally true that future Congresses could work the same dark magic on the FairTax by seeking to curry voter favor by exempting this or that item from the FairTax.

For that reason we're going to try to impose a supermajority requirement before Congress can exclude or exempt any good or service from the FairTax. But your role will be crucial in ensuring that the FairTax isn't gutted by Washington. Income tax increases are typically sold to the public by promising that they will only affect the top 2 percent of income earners—always a winning argument at the polls. The FairTax will impact everyone equally. Any exemptions would end up raising the FairTax rate for everyone. We're counting on you to withhold your vote from politicians who demonstrate a willingness to tamper with this very delicate system by exempting items whose purchasers happen to have the clout to pay for a lobbyist.

Back to the numbers: In 2005, total personal consumption exceeded personal taxable income by more than 70 percent. Total personal consumption was $8.7 trillion, taxable income $5.1 trillion. Seems as though that larger base would be safer from erosion than the smaller one, doesn't it? You'd think that a larger base—a base that touches everyone equally—would be less likely to pick winners and losers, wouldn't you? The Nobel Prize–winning economist Milton Friedman thought so. When asked by the President's Advisory Panel on Federal Tax Reform what kind of tax base would be best protected from erosion, he replied, "[I]t seems to me that . . . if you have a system in which there were no exemptions, no special deductions, [it] would be . . . most likely to stay the same from year to year and not have the interventions." Sound like a certain tax system you've heard us talk about?

Additionally, for decades the consumption base has remained much more predictable, in both good times and bad, than the income base has. The legislative changes occurring constantly at the state and federal levels make it difficult to look at raw tax revenue numbers and determine if they rose or fell based on economic conditions or legislative changes. To make our point about the stability of the consumption base, then, we turn to the Rockefeller Institute of Government—the public policy research arm of the State University of New York—which has spent years analyzing changes in state revenues across the nation. The chart below, based on that analysis, reflects the change—in percentage points from the previous quarter—of both total state personal income tax (PIT) receipts and total sales tax receipts for all states. The Rockefeller Institute has gone so far as to adjust these numbers to eliminate the effect of legislative changes in tax rates and/or exemptions affecting the tax base, and so on. The chart reflects exclusively economic conditions, which is exactly what we want to measure.

Quarterly Percent Change in State Tax Revenues: 1995–2007

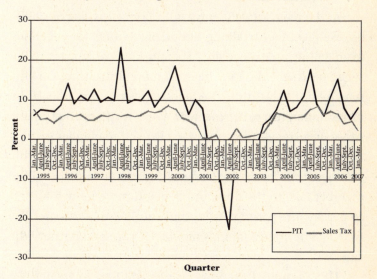

Look at the line reflecting sales tax. While the personal income tax (PIT) is spiking regularly, the sales tax line is much more stable. But what about the giant collapse in the middle of the PIT line? You're absolutely right: those are the quarters following September 11, 2001. While Americans' income was dramatically affected, you can see that their consumption—while still affected—remained relatively stable. Why? Because consumption comes from three sources: income, savings, and borrowing. Stating the obvious, income comes only from income. Our point? FairTax opponents will tell you that the consumption base, the base for the national sales tax, isn't stable and can't be trusted—but in reality it's the income tax base that's unstable and can't be trusted. The consumption base is much more predictable.

And remember: When we talk about the value of stability, we're not just talking about preventing tax revenues from falling unexpectedly. The prospect of tax revenues rising unexpectedly may be even more distressing. Do you remember the last time the federal government brought in more money than it expected? Well, it's happened many times over the past twenty years. Do you remember getting a special refund? I didn't think so. On the contrary: if you watched the debate in Congress, you saw member after member take to the floor and demand more money for his or her favorite program from the "surplus" that was coming in. To paraphrase a famous movie, "If you send it, they will spend it."

There's more. It appears that in addition to greater tax base stability, states that have no personal income tax (relying instead on sales taxes) have faster-growing economies than income tax states. If that isn't a selling point for the FairTax, we can't imagine what is. Personal income, population, and jobs all grew faster in the nine states[9] with no income tax than in the nine states with the highest personal income tax rates.

Economic Indicators: No-Income-Tax States versus High-Income-Tax States [10]
(Cumulative percentage change from 1994 to 2004)

State Economic Indicators	Nine States with No Personal Income Tax	Nine States with High Personal Income Tax Rates
Gross state output growth	79.7%	62.5%
Personal income growth	77.2%	60.2%
Personal income per capita	50.9%	48.7%
Population growth	17.8%	6.4%
Job growth	22.9%	12.8%
Unemployment rate	5.1%	5.2%

We know how much you like charts and graphs; go ahead and spend a little time with that one. Just more evidence of the economic advantages of a consumption tax over an income tax. Is it sinking in yet?

---

9. The lucky residents of Alaska, Florida, Nevada, New Hampshire, South Dakota, Tennessee, Texas, Washington, and Wyoming do not face a personal state income tax.

10. Source: Arduin, Laffer & Moore Econometrics, "A Macroeconomic Analysis of the FairTax Proposal," July 2006.

Disadvantages? Maybe one. It makes politicians less powerful.

Criticism: The only way to keep the FairTax rate low is to tax services—but experience shows that state sales taxes on services haven't worked.

When giving a speech on the FairTax some years ago in Washington, D.C., to a group of doctors from California, we were taken by the positive response of the doctors. They applauded, they cheered—until one woman got a startled look on her face and jumped out of her seat. "You expect me to tax my patients?" she said.

Our response: "What makes you think you're so special? All your neighbors tax the source of their income to support the state. Why shouldn't you?"

She never got over that exchange, but her colleagues did. Doctors, like most service providers, understand how much of their costs are labor costs and how much they pay in payroll taxes on behalf of their employees—and from there it's just a short leap for them to realize how much their costs of equipment are inflated by the embedded costs of the current tax system. With a little explanation, most of them come to recognize that they're taxing their patients already. The only difference between the current system and the FairTax is that the tax they currently levy on their patients is embedded—hidden—in their fees. With the FairTax, those taxes will be clearly delineated as a part of the fee they charge. The cost to the patient remains essentially the same . . . only now the patients come away with an understanding of the cost elements of their medical care.

Doctors and other professionals have also described for us just how much time and money they spend on tax planning. Some spend tens of thousands of dollars setting up legal tax avoidance schemes, and then pay thousands of dollars each year in maintenance costs. Many of them see the FairTax as an opportunity to decrease the payments they seek from their patients and clients without affecting their personal incomes. And the record-keeping involved shouldn't be much worse than the income and payroll tax reports they're burdened with today. Under the FairTax, they simply need to keep track of their business-to-business purchases, and the amount of gross sales and the tax collected. That's it. And they won't even be paying these taxes—their patients will.

We didn't make the decision to tax services capriciously. We believe as a matter of principle that government shouldn't pick winners and losers. We have no right to decide that those who make their living selling goods should put out the time and effort to collect revenues for the government, while those who sell services can just sit back and enjoy it. Under the current tax system, both these elements of our economy carry the burden of embedded taxes. The FairTax should not completely untax one sector, the service sector, while taxing the other.

Today, personal consumption of services constitutes nearly 60 percent of national personal consumption and 42 percent of our economy. Compare this to 1950, when services only accounted for a third of personal consumption and 22 percent of our economy. The graph below shows how the services portion of expenditures has climbed steadily and the goods portion has fallen since 1950.

Composition of Personal Consumption Expenditures (PCE)

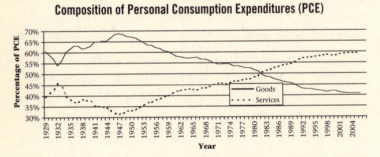

Source: *Computations based on Bureau of Economic Analysis NIPA Table 2.3.5.*

Of course, all of this raises the question of Internet commerce. Just as we believe that services should be taxed, we propose that a procedure should be set up in the Treasury Department to collect taxes on Internet and catalog sales, remitting the state and local governments' share to them. You may not be aware of this, but it's perfectly legal to tax Internet sales today at the state level. For practical reasons, however, this is done by only the largest companies. State governments lost about $23 billion in tax collections on Internet sales in 2001, and that number is growing dramatically each year. By 2008, it is estimated to be almost $34 billion.[11]

Okay—we understand that you like your Internet tax-free zone. The idea of taxing Internet sales probably has you ready to throw this book across the room. Remember, though, that the FairTax isn't about picking economic winners and losers. Fairness means that all commerce is treated equally. We're not looking for new ways to tax, but it just isn't fair to put our neighbor, who builds a building to sell books in our community, hires our kids, participates in our community, votes in our elections, and attends our places of worship at a 23 percent disadvantage to an Internet bookseller.

Nevertheless, the fact that so many states with sales taxes exempt services from collecting those taxes makes this seem like a big step for service providers and consumers alike. We agree that it's an important step, of course—but we'd like to demonstrate that it won't be difficult to do.

While a tax on your doctor's services may seem unusual to many of you, a state sales tax on other services is not. A Federation of Tax Administrators survey found that, on average, 55 of 164 service categories are taxed at the state level, with business and other services the most frequently taxed and computer and professional services the least

---

11. Donald Bruce and William F. Fox, "State and Local Tax Revenue Losses from E-Commerce: Estimates as of July 2004," *State Tax Notes* 33, no. 7, August 16, 2004.

taxed. Hawaii and New Mexico have broad-based sales taxes that include almost all services (160 and 156, respectively). In fact, the survey found that five states already tax half or more of the 164 identified service categories.[12] So, while most state sales taxes have lagged behind the general trend of the U.S. economy moving away from goods production and toward higher value service production, the experience of the more forward-looking states shows us that change is not only possible but available today.

Whoa, you might say. What about that disaster in Florida a few years back when it tried to institute a tax on services? That's a good question, particularly for folks who just read the headlines. It's true that Florida faced an uprising from doctors, dentists, lawyers, and other service providers when it imposed a tax on services—so much so that it ultimately had to repeal the tax. But the lesson of the Florida experience isn't that taxes on services won't work—it's that uniformity is key.

You see, beyond the simple service taxes, Florida also tried something no other state has: to impose a tax on media outlets for the value of media services (advertising) they provided in Florida. Confused? So were the media outlets.

Here's how it was supposed to work. Let's say McDonald's comes out with a new "two all-beef patties, special

---

12. Federation of Tax Administrators, "2004 Survey on State Taxation of Services"; available at www.taxadmin.org/fta/pub/services/services04.html.

sauce" campaign it wants to release nationwide. Under its short-lived plan, Florida would have taxed McDonald's on the share of that campaign that came into Florida. How would that have been calculated? Well, McDonald's would have needed to get in touch will all of the print, radio, and TV outlets in Florida, determine how many people viewed the ad, and pay a tax on that. Good grief! And they say the FairTax is crazy. No wonder the Florida service tax was repealed.

But let's peel the onion back a layer or two. First, Florida was trying to impose a tax on advertising in Florida on businesses that weren't based in Florida. That's like trying to impose a Florida sales tax on goods purchased by Floridians but sold by Internet companies from across the nation: it's hard to do, and it places a special burden on the company to come up with a special Florida solution.

Second, Florida placed the sales tax on business-to-business transactions as well as consumer sales. Think back to our "embedded taxes in a loaf of bread" example. Florida was imposing a tax on every one of those service steps— and then again on the final sale. Think about how many additional transactions would have had to be monitored there and how all those taxes would have cascaded through those layers to the final consumer.

Finally, both of those missteps hit the advertising and media industries. Hmmm . . . let's think about this for a moment. Do those industries have any special tools at their disposal for influencing public opinion?

The Florida services tax never had a chance.

The FairTax is completely different. It's a uniform national tax, making collection simple and easy. It *replaces* other burdensome taxes, rather than adding another layer of unpleasantness or a new cost.

The FairTax doesn't tax business-to-business transactions. All those dozens of steps involved in making bread are exempt; only the final sale to the consumer is taxed. And it doesn't pick winner and losers. It applies to absolutely all consumer purchases, so no one industry will feel advantaged or disadvantaged.

This is just yet another example of the importance of distinguishing between "a sales tax" and the FairTax. Have there been examples of disastrous state sales taxes? Absolutely. Have the researchers behind the FairTax learned from those and created thoughtful solutions?

Count on it.

Criticism: The FairTax keeps the rate low by taxing government consumption. But taxing the government doesn't make sense— and it won't work.

The FairTax treats all governments—federal, state, and local—as individual consumers. Under the plan, all government purchases of labor, supplies, or services would be subject to the FairTax.

Why would you tax the government? For this one, let's turn to the President's Advisory Panel on Federal Tax Reform, which considered the same question during its consideration of the VAT, another consumption tax. The panel came to the same conclusion that we did: "The rationale for this treatment is to prevent federal, state, or local government from having an advantage over the private sector in areas where the two might compete to supply similar products."[13] Doesn't that sound like a worthy goal to you? Why would we want to use tax policy to give government a leg up on the private sector?

The reason behind this provision is entirely a matter of principle: governments shouldn't use the taxes paid by taxpayers to compete against the very taxpayers who support them.

Many states have prison industries, which raise money, for example, by selling cleaning chemicals to other government offices. They take the taxes paid by private chemical manufacturers to feed and house the prison population, who works for them at virtually no labor cost, and then compete against the very companies that pay those taxes, thereby subsidizing their competition.

By the same token, many cities sell electricity or natural gas to their citizens. They go to the voters bragging about how they are keeping property taxes low because they make a profit on the services. But they do so because they're being subsidized by the property taxes taken from the businesses they compete with. And they pass statutes that outlaw competition.

In Georgia, a federally owned organization called the

---

13. President's Advisory Panel on Federal Tax Reform, Final Report, November 2005, p. 198.

Southeastern Power Authority (SEPA) provides electricity to a large swath of citizens in eastern Georgia. During the 1995 Republican takeover in Washington, a proposal was put forth to auction the facility off to the private sector. The uproar from the citizens and some of their representatives was huge. It became clear to many that if a private electricity provider owned the facility, electricity rates would move to competitive market rates. If that happened, the rates would rise. It took no time at all to understand this arrangement: the rates were being subsidized by the federal taxpayer.

If you begin with the common, entirely rational assumption (as we do) that no government can provide goods and services to anyone as efficiently as a private business, why not encourage governments to get out of the competitive marketplace for any services not uniquely the province of government?

It's easy to see, as the president's tax panel did, the huge competitive advantage that governments would have over the private sector if they were exempt from paying the FairTax. By taxing governments' purchases of labor and supplies, we limit the competitive advantage that they have over private businesses, the very businesses that create the wealth from which governments derive taxes.

Would that increase the cost of government? Let's explore that question.

First, governments at all levels already pay taxes. The income and payroll taxes that government deducts from the checks of government employees—plus the employer's portion of the payroll tax—are all remitted to the federal government out of government coffers. The same embedded taxes that exist today in the goods and services you buy at the retail level are present in the cost of goods and services purchased by governments. Just as with personal consumption, the equilibrium between increased take-home pay and reduced prices from eliminated embedded tax costs would insulate governments from increased costs. If prices go down, the spending side of the government ledger benefits. If prices don't go down because take-home pay goes up instead, the revenue side of the government ledger would benefit from increased consumer spending.

One more thing: Who would benefit from government paying the FairTax? Why, that would be government. Just where is the problem here?

Criticism: I've seen conflicting claims. Will the FairTax drive prices up or down?

Here's a claim that has taken on mythical proportion in the anti-FairTax literature: "When the 22 percent embedded cost of the IRS is driven out of the price system and replaced by the 23 percent tax, your cost of living will go up about 1 percent—but you'll get to keep your whole check. The average income earner will get about a 50 percent increase in take home pay. That more than makes up for the 1 percent increase in the cost."

You've seen this sentiment before: we took it on earlier, in the "Myths About the FairTax" chapter. But now that we're into the real meat of the book, let's go after it one more time.

Can everything in the statement above be true? Nope—not at the same time, not in the first year of the FairTax.

As we often note, the payroll tax and personal income tax withholding account for much of the embedded cost of the IRS. If abolished by the FairTax, these two taxes could not be retained by the employer to reduce the cost of the product *and* given to the employee to increase his take-home pay. That would be using the same dollars twice.

But can we even be sure that those dollars would be used for some combination of reducing the cost of the product or increasing your pay? Absolutely—competition will guarantee it. And the result is that America's standard of living will stay roughly the same[14] even though America

---

14. The value of an hour of work will continue to buy the same amount of goods before and after the FairTax is enacted, even though the actual dollar value of that hour of work or that basket of goods may move up or down. Over time, however, America's standard of living will rise relative to the pre-FairTax system. The economics of the FairTax—which would drive increased investment—will ensure it. But for the purposes of this chapter, it's important to know that even though we cannot predict with certainty whether paychecks and prices will rise, fall, or do a little of both, we can predict with certainty that an hour of work will still buy an hour's worth of goods.

will be seeing the full and true cost of its tax system for the very first time.

Here's what's likely to happen: Most employers will give their employees a gross check that includes the dollars that used to be withheld for income and payroll taxes. As Alan Greenspan has told us, "Wages are sticky things." People who have agreed to work for a given pay will expect to earn that pay.

Depending on the employment rate and the availability of a competent workforce, some employers will give their workers the portion of the payroll tax that the company pays on the employee's behalf. After all, that too is part of the cost of that person's employment. Most will try not to do that, and the result will depend on the workforce.

What about the reduction in the cost of goods and services? For the sake of argument, let's assume the worst—that at first every company will try to keep prices at the current level and increase their profits. As we've discussed, they'll never succeed: competition will drive those costs out of the system. If the company tries to keep the portion of the payroll tax that it pays on behalf of employees, that cost will be driven out of the price of the product or service.

It's important to note that the 22 percent cost of the IRS that's embedded in the price system we're talking about doesn't include the cost of complying with the code. The entire floors of some companies' offices are occupied by tax specialists. Some companies have entire floors occupied by IRS employees year-round. The billions of dollars that go to pay for those specialists—including the billions spent just calculating the tax implications of a business decision—will quickly come out of the price system.

For most workers—whose average withholding is 25 percent for income taxes and approximately 8 percent for payroll taxes—there will be a substantial increase in take-home pay. When you add the prebate to this increase in take-home pay, everyone will benefit from an increase in purchasing power—and that's just in year one.

Over the long term, the worker's pocket will grow ever fuller—regardless of what happens to prices. For example, one macroeconomic study of the FairTax—a study that assumed that the employer's share of the payroll tax is the only tax savings that will be used to lower prices—estimated that prices would rise by 24.8 percent but wages would rise by 27.4 percent, more than compensating for the increase in prices. By these calculations, disposable income is expected to increase by 1.7 percent.[15]

And of course it's important to remember that you'll be paying the FairTax only on whatever portion of your income you decide to spend. Investments and savings will escape the FairTax.

---

15. Arduin, Laffer & Moore Econometrics, "A Macroeconomic Analysis of the FairTax Proposal," Americans for Fair Taxation Research Monograph, July 2006.

FairTax Simulation Model Results[16]

Cumulative Growth over Current System	Year 1	Year 2	Year 3	Year 4	Year 5	Year 10
Gross domestic product	2.4%	5.2%	7.0%	8.2%	9.0%	11.3%
Employment	3.5%	5.7%	7.0%	7.7%	8.2%	9.0%
Domestic investment	33.0%	35.4%	36.9%	38.0%	38.8%	41.2%
Income from employment (wages)	27.4%	31.8%	34.5%	36.4%	37.7%	41.2%
Consumption	2.4%	4.1%	5.8%	7.1%	8.1%	11.7%
Disposable personal income (adjusted for changes in the price level)	1.7%	4.5%	6.4%	7.7%	8.7%	11.8%

Units are scaled to 2004 GDP = 1.00. Capital and labor are set to equal constant shares of 0.3 and 0.7, respectively.

It's critically important to understand a study like this one, because the anti-FairTax lobby is always arguing that the FairTax will raise prices by almost 25 percent. That sounds scary—and this study agrees with them!

But it's only scary until you look again—and realize

---

16. Ibid. The complete analysis can be found at www.fairtax.org/PDF/MacroeconomicAnalysisofFairTax.pdf.

that workers' paychecks will be increased by an even greater amount!

You can see how easy it is to "disprove" the merits of the FairTax using this study. If you hear some politician saying that the FairTax will raise taxes by more than 20 percent, what's the average listener more likely to do—question his math or go home trembling in horror at the prospect of paying that much more on every trip to the store? Of course, the demagogue will somehow forget to cover two important details: the prebate and the fact that your personal income will increase more than the prices! Remember that 1.7 percent increase in year one? By year ten, this study suggests, that disposable income may be almost 12 percent higher for working Americans than it would have been under the current tax system.

You see? Even the most alarming economic studies of the FairTax still paint a winning picture for American wage earners. What do we have to lose?

Studies like this lead us to conclude that it truly doesn't matter whether prices rise or wages fall (to current take-home pay levels) or if some combination of the two occurs. In every case, American workers would have more purchasing power in the domestic marketplace in a FairTax world than they do in today.

Criticism: Tax evasion under the FairTax will cripple our economy.

First, let's admit that even with the FairTax there will be cheating. We're Americans, after all: cheating on taxes is a time-honored letter sport in our school of hard knocks. But will tax cheating be any worse under the FairTax than it is today? We think not!

We've been told from the beginning that a tax rate as high as 23 percent will cause huge evasion problems. We hear it most often from people in the Treasury Department, who will go to any extreme to prevent a change in the current system. Is it any surprise that people who owe their very jobs to the complexity of our present tax system fight simplification? (Remember, even if they should leave the government, many of these people may be expecting to spend the rest of their lives as lobbyists gaming the current system.)

Let's look at the state of tax cheating under the current system. In 2001, the last year for which information is available, the IRS reports that it collected $345 billion less than it was owed—or about 16 percent of all that was owed, a figure known as "the tax gap."

The IRS is always quick to produce statistics detailing the shortfall in the collection of income taxes. It doesn't seem quite as eager to estimate the shortfall in tax payments from income earned by the underground economy. We're told that they just can't figure out a way to come up with such an estimate. Are you following us here? The IRS, in other words, is happy to let us know how much money it's losing to those who cheat on their tax returns—but they'd prefer not to talk about how much it's losing to the underground economy.

One of the ingenious by-products of the FairTax is that

participants in the underground economy can't escape it. They may rake in millions of dollars through gambling, drugs, or other illegal activities. They may create some very impressive bank accounts with the money they've made off the books. But when they go out to spend those dollars—whether on jewelry, Jaguars, or junk food—they'll be paying the FairTax

Might we suggest that when you combine the "tax gap" (which the IRS does estimate) with the lost tax revenue from the underground economy (which it doesn't), the total lost tax revenue dwarfs any realistic estimate of cheating under the FairTax?

There's another point to be made: cheating under the FairTax would be more difficult than cheating on an income tax return. Why? Because with the FairTax, it takes two to cheat.

It's not that difficult to lie on your tax return. You just enter a false figure, sign, and file. You don't have to tell anyone, not even your spouse. Your risk of being audited is less than 1 percent. With the FairTax, on the other hand, you need two people—a seller and a purchaser—to conspire to cheat, and each of them is risking jail to do so. We don't know how many of your friends would be willing to risk jail to save you 23 cents on a dollar, but we have none.

And when you look at who'll be collecting this tax, the chances of drumming up a conspiracy suddenly look even worse. In America, .03 percent of all of America's companies—688 companies, to be exact—sell 48.5 percent of all of the merchandise. Those companies aren't going to help you cheat; there's simply too much at stake. Data also show that 3.6 percent of all of America's companies—92,334 firms—collectively make 85.7 percent of all sales.[17] They aren't going to help you cheat either. It's more important for the owners of these companies to stay in business and out of jail than it is to help you avoid paying the FairTax.

What about services? Isn't this where most of the cheating will occur? Is the lawn guy really going to pay 23 percent to the feds?

When it comes to the services sector, the fact is that 1.2 percent of all businesses make approximately 80 percent of the sales in the service sector. They have too much to lose to risk helping you cheat. Even if the FairTax were paid only by these few companies, we would still have a better collection rate than the IRS currently has with the income tax.

Of the remaining 96 percent of the retail companies and nearly 99 percent of the service companies, most will be honest and collect the tax. Some, of course, will not. The fact remains that the collection rate for the FairTax will be better than the collection rate for the income tax. Add to this the fact that we'll also be collecting the FairTax from the underground economy and from illegal aliens—taxes

---

17. These numbers are truly astounding, aren't they? You can see them for yourself in the Census Bureau's Economic Census, conducted every five years. These numbers come from the 2002 Census. The 2007 Census data will be available in 2009.

that aren't even anticipated or quantified by the current tax regime—and you can see how the numbers stack up.

So where *will* the cheating come from? Since the biggest problem in collections in the income tax regime comes from sole proprietors, we'd guess that same business sector will creatively avoid the FairTax. The guy who comes to fix your roof may collect the tax from you but not remit it. But the vast majority of small businesses, the ones with business licenses to protect, will collect and remit the FairTax so they don't lose their license or go to jail. We believe the numbers for compliance and avoidance dramatically favor the FairTax.

So there it is: most of the FairTax money will be collected by big companies that have no interest in cheating, and the lower marginal rates will mean that small companies will have less interest in cheating.

And then there's one more biggie: enforcement.

The FairTax takes current individual taxpayers out of the tax collection and payment business altogether. Just how many people would that be? Try 165 million. That's 165 million people who at present need to be watched, and perhaps audited, by the IRS to ensure compliance. With the FairTax, we'll have about 25 million businesses to watch instead of 165 million taxpayers. Suddenly the challenges of enforcement are starting to look a lot easier, aren't they? Further, the states and the feds—at least in the forty-five states that have sales taxes—will be looking at the same companies.

Maybe we're just too straight and narrow, but it seems

to us that the idea of cheating under the FairTax is more like a red herring than a real problem.[18]

Criticism: The prebate is a giant government handout. It would be better just to exempt things like groceries and medical care.

Many people have approached us with the argument that we should do away with the prebate and simply exempt necessities from the FairTax. They dismiss the prebate as very expensive to administer, as the largest entitlement ever passed. And we can understand why many people don't like the idea of every household in the United States getting a monthly check from the government. Heck, we don't like the sound of that either.

But is the prebate a handout? Hardly. We start with the assumption that every household is going to spend what it needs to every month to provide for the basic necessities. We believe that the government should acknowledge and honor the need of every household, rich or poor, to cover the cost of its basic needs before it starts funding government. The FairTax prebate would no more be a welfare program than are the standard deduction and personal

---

18. We should note here that implementation of the FairTax doesn't mean complete annihilation of the IRS. Even after the Fair-Tax, the IRS should be expected to stick around until it has completed its one remaining mandate: collecting taxes still due from the era of the income tax. Passage of the FairTax shouldn't be viewed as an amnesty for past tax cheats.

exemptions we have under the current income tax system. To disagree with this approach is to believe that the government should have the first claim on household income—a claim superior to that household's need to provide for its own sustenance. That's an America none of us wants.

The critics of the prebate somehow never seem to mention that the current income tax system doles out about $456 billion *more* to "favored" taxpayers than the FairTax prebate. The FairTax prebate is an advance rebate of taxes that would be paid on spending up to the poverty level based on family size. The cumulative prebate cost is estimated by the Beacon Hill Institute of Suffolk University in Boston to be $489 billion per year (assuming 100 percent participation).[19] Compare that to the $945 billion cost of income tax deductions, tax preferences, loopholes, credits, and favors that we have under the current system (as estimated by the Joint Committee on Taxation).[20] Would you really prefer to keep the almost trillion-dollar cost of today's convoluted system in place while rejecting a prebate that would cost half as much and would treat all Americans equally? Does that sound like a good move to you?

"How would it be administered?" you ask. "Wouldn't

---

19. David G. Tuerck, Jonathan Haughton, Paul Bachman, and Alfonso Sanchez-Penalver, "A Comparison of the FairTax Base and Rate with Other National Tax Reform Proposals," Beacon Hill Institute at Suffolk University, February 2007.
20. Congressional Research Service, "Tax Expenditures: Trends and Critiques," September 13, 2006.

that make for an unmanageable amount of paperwork?" Nope. For one thing, we don't envision the prebate ever being a check. The federal government has been moving toward electronic transfers for years. For example, more than 99 percent of all federal salary payments and 83 percent of all Social Security payments today are made by electronic transfer directly into the recipients' bank accounts.[21] Electronic transfers save the government 80 cents per recipient compared to the cost of sending a check. Issuing a paper check costs the federal government $0.89. An electronic transfer costs about one-tenth that amount—and it occurs almost instantaneously. The prebate could be distributed to millions of households with little more than the click of a mouse.

The prebate could also be distributed through a debit card provided to each qualified household. Each month the amount of that family's prebate could be electronically transferred to the card.[22] A 1996 federal law required that paper food stamps be converted to an electronic format.

---

21. See www.fms.treas.gov/eft/reports/payment_volume_FY07.pdf.
22. Interestingly enough, some major credit card companies have expressed an interest in setting up a system whereby they would administer the FairTax prebate for their credit card holders. The government would transfer the funds to the credit card company every month, and on the first day of each month the appropriate prebate would be credited to each holder's account. What's more, these credit card companies have even broached the idea of paying the federal government a fee for the privilege of handling these prebates.

Today, all fifty states use electronic cards to distribute 99.8 percent of all food "stamp" benefits.[23]

What about the argument that exempting groceries and health care would be easier and fairer? One member of Congress has suggested that we identify certain products for exemption—that we should exclude potatoes, for example, but not potato chips. We agree with him that potatoes are better for you than potato chips, but this fellow missed one of the main points of the FairTax: chips, French fries, or smashed potatoes—it's your choice. The government should have no place in that decision. The government's role should be limited to collecting taxes to raise needed revenue, not controlling our lifestyle choices.

Furthermore, providing tax relief through the prebate makes the administration of the tax much more efficient and keeps compliance costs at a minimum for retailers and service providers. The greatest complaint businesses have about state sales taxes is how complex all the exemptions are and how costly it is to administer them.

Exclusions and exemptions? Isn't that what's made our current system such a chaotic mess? Politicians have been picking winners and losers for decades. You favor certain activities or interests with tax deductions and credits. Let the consumers pick the winners and losers. Government needs to butt out.

Here's another point for those who would scrap the prebate for a hideously complicated system of exclusions

---

23. See www.fns.usda.gov/fsp/ebt/FAQ.HTM.

and exemptions: Personal consumption of food represents about a sixth of the economy. Health care and services represent another sixth. To exempt them would take about a third of the economy off the table, and the ultimate tax rate would be too high to be practicable.

Exempting necessities would also give the lobbyists a new job. They would be hired by every interest group in the country to convince Congress that their interest group is clearly essential and should also be exempted. Once the dam breaks, the FairTax just won't work.

It's clear—even without those millions of dollars' worth of research—that the prebate is the best method for untaxing every household right up to the poverty level. Fair and simple. Isn't it about time we had that in a tax code?

Criticism: Just repealing and replacing the income tax code seems difficult enough. Isn't the FairTax overreaching by going after the payroll tax too?

FairTax aside, something must be done about our current income tax. Any fair analysis of what the income tax has become will show that at the very least it is a threat to economic liberty and at worse a threat to our Republic. By no rational set of criteria could the current income tax be described as anything approximating "fair."

Take a look at the chart below. As you'll see, 40 percent of our population is actually on the take! The bottom 50 percent of all income earners pay just 3.4 percent of the income taxes collected. In 1986 that figure was 6.7 percent.

The trend is clearly going in the wrong direction. We're moving steadily to a situation where the majority of income earners in this country, or the majority of voters (however you want to label it), will be paying no income tax whatsoever. This is a trend that has been nurtured by Democrats and Republicans alike.

Who Pays the Federal Income Tax? (by percentage of total tax paid)

Source: Chart created by the authors using data compiled by the Congressional

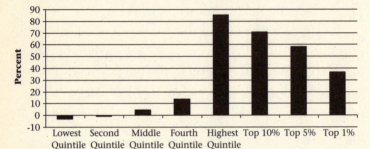

Budget Office. The chart represents the percentage of the total federal income tax burden paid by each of the income classes shown. The data come from tax year 2004, the most recent year for which data are available.

Is that chart enough to convince you? Do you see where we're going? We've already reached the point where the overwhelming majority of taxes are paid by a small minority of the taxpayers. How long will it be before we get to the point where the majority pay no income taxes at all? How will the majority react when a political candidate tells them, "Vote for my candidate, and he'll make you pay income taxes"?

There's a quote that has been most commonly attributed to Alexander Fraser Tytler in *The Decline and Fall of the Athenian Republic*: "A democracy cannot exist as a permanent form of government. It can only exist until the voters discover that they can vote themselves [generous benefits] from the public treasury. From that moment on, the majority always votes for the candidates promising them the most benefits from the public treasury, with the result that a democracy always collapses over loose fiscal policy, always followed by a dictatorship." Sound familiar? Benjamin Franklin is said to have sounded the same alarm: "When the people find they can vote themselves money, that will herald the end of the republic." We do not take these warnings lightly.

But solving the problem above by reforming or replacing only the income tax and ignoring payroll taxes will translate into a huge tax increase on the bottom 40 percent of income earners. More reformers give up their pursuit at this point.

What we're saying here is that Americans have a troubling tendency to focus on the income tax. When was the last time you were sitting around the dinner table and the topic of payroll taxes came up? Well, shame on you—and us all—because the payroll tax is the largest tax most of us pay. In fact—and read this carefully—*the payroll tax brings in almost as much money every year as the personal in-*

come tax does. In 2004, the payroll tax actually raised *more* money for the federal government than the personal income tax did.

So why do Americans spend so much time talking about the income tax and so little talking about the payroll tax? Keep this question in the front of your mind as we approach some additional criticisms of the FairTax.

Most of these criticisms compare the FairTax (or any garden-variety sales tax) to the income tax and then proceed to hastily drawn conclusions. Well, the FairTax is not a garden-variety sales tax. If you're going to compare the FairTax to anything, you must compare it to both the current income tax *and* the current payroll tax. The FairTax would abolish and replace *both*! While we're at it, you should also throw in the corporate income tax, which would also be replaced by the FairTax.

What difference does it make? A huge difference—because one of the most common and talked-about ways to look at a tax code is through a single-year distributional analysis. Now, we don't think that's the best way to view a code—and many scholars and economists agree with us—but we'll put that aside for now. The chart we included above was a single-year distributional analysis of the personal income tax—the tax everyone talks about, writes about, and worries about. But what would a chart of the payroll tax look like? Here's your answer.

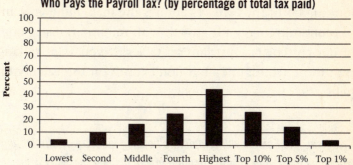

Who Pays the Payroll Tax? (by percentage of total tax paid)

As you can see, the payroll tax is still progressive—those who earn more pay more—but you don't see the negative numbers at the lower income levels as you do with the income tax, and you don't see the incredibly high numbers for the high income levels as you do with the income tax. This is important, since the payroll tax takes almost as much money from Americans as the income tax does. And since most of us pay more in payroll taxes than we do in income taxes, when it comes time to ask, "How will the FairTax affect my pocketbook?" the fact that the FairTax would abolish both the income tax and the payroll tax becomes critically important.

So, in logistical terms, would it be easier just to reform the income tax? Probably. That's been tried before with other consumption tax plans. But real reform—real change—is impossible in the context of the income tax alone. And since the payroll tax is just as heavy a burden as the income tax, it doesn't make economic sense to try to solve one without addressing the other. By reforming both, the FairTax captures the maximum amount of economic energy for growth with minimum disruption of our current tax distribution tables. If you want to disrupt those tables, fine—but don't count on the FairTax to help.

Criticism: The FairTax will cripple the housing industry by eliminating the home mortgage interest deduction and placing the FairTax on new home purchases.

First, let's deal with the argument about the home mortgage interest deduction.

There's a very respected syndicated talk-show host on the West Coast who is often asked by his callers if he supports the FairTax. He answers that he does not because it would take away the mortgage interest deduction. Virtually every time he says this on his program we get anguished e-mails from listeners begging for us to contact this talk-show host and set him straight on the mortgage interest issue.

This is both good news and bad news. The bad news is that there is a widely respected talk-show host who, quite frankly, doesn't have a clue in the world what he is talking about. The good news is that there are thousands of listeners who immediately recognize that fact.

Perhaps we can cut to the chase by asking you a couple of questions:

1. Would the home mortgage interest deduction be of any value to you if you didn't owe any income taxes?[24]

2. If you walked into a grocery store with a coupon for 25 percent off bread, would you be angry if you found out they were giving bread away that day?

You see what we're driving at: the home mortgage interest deduction is meaningless *if you don't pay income taxes.* You may be surprised to learn that about 70 percent of households that pay income taxes don't take advantage of the mortgage interest deduction anyway. The deduction means nothing to them because they don't itemize deductions on their tax returns.

Proponents of the home mortgage interest deduction like to claim that it exists to help the middle class own homes . . . but they rarely provide the data on who really benefits from the $69.4 billion tax deduction.[25] Remember the mortgage deduction example from when we were talking about earmarks earlier? A close look reveals that little of

---

24. If you answered yes, put this book down now. We can be of no further help to you. Then again, you could hang in there for some more pithy and entertaining footnotes.

25. Joint Committee on Taxation, "Estimates of Federal Tax Expenditures Fiscal Years 2006–2010," Prepared for the House Ways and Means Committee and the Senate Finance Committee, April 25, 2006, p. 33.

that benefit goes to low- and middle-income families. According to IRS data, more than half of the taxpayers claiming the deduction earn less than $30,000, but they collectively receive less than 10 percent of the total mortgage interest deduction benefit. Likewise, the 71 percent of filers with incomes less than $50,000 received only a quarter of the total tax deduction. Perhaps this home mortgage interest deduction isn't the middle-class savior some claim it to be.

This one may take a little time for you to digest, because so many people are accustomed to praising the effectiveness of the home mortgage interest deduction. You won't be alone if you admit you were fooled. In fact, when the President's Advisory Panel on Federal Tax Reform released its proposals for reform, the one proposal it made that no one argued with was restructuring the home mortgage interest deduction to ensure that the dominant portion of the benefit would go to low- and middle-income Americans. Like so many others, however, even House Speaker Nancy Pelosi misunderstands who receives the giveaway that is the home mortgage interest deduction today. She railed against the panel's report, claiming that it "would demolish the building blocks middle-class Americans use to reach the American dream. . . . The president's tax panel would severely limit the mortgage-interest deduction." Well, she's right; the panel did propose limiting the deduction, but not for anyone in the middle class. The panel's target was limiting the benefit for those with seven-figure homes or second homes in vacation locales—the theory being that if you have either, you probably don't need a government subsidy to help you with your interest payments.

Let's talk some more about the effect of the FairTax on the sale of new homes.

Even though the FairTax makes the mortgage interest deduction irrelevant, not only will housing be *more* affordable, but home buyers will have more money to use in buying a home. Here's why: roughly three-quarters of home sales involve *existing* homes, which wouldn't be taxed under the FairTax. And unlike today, taxpayers could use untaxed earnings to buy used homes. Is this sinking in? If you buy a previously owned home there's no FairTax—and what's more, you're buying that home with what would today be called pretax money!

Realtors sell houses based on how much income a buyer brings home each month. They use the mortgage interest deduction to show the potential buyer that the tax advantage will increase his or her take-home pay. So let's say a buyer makes $60,000 per year and takes home about $3,800 per month. By using the tax calculation he or she may be able to get the take-home pay up to $4,000 per month. The extra two hundred bucks a month may be just enough to convince the prospect that he or she can afford the new home.

Now, what if that Realtor could somehow increase the prospective home buyer's income by $1,200 a month instead of $200? Do we see an even larger home in the picture here? Plus, FairTax studies show that interest rates could decline by as much as 24 percent with the FairTax. That new home is getting bigger all the time, and now it may even have a swimming pool out back!

There is one group out there that won't see the good news in the scenario we're painting for you. What are Washington lobbyists going to do if home buyers can buy houses with untaxed earnings and if the mortgage interest deduction becomes a needless relic of a past tax system? Well, let's just say they aren't going to be proposing toasts to the FairTax at their favorite K Street watering holes.

You can see how the advantages from the FairTax are starting to add up. Mortgage debt will be paid at a 25 percent lower interest rate, and, unlike in the current tax code, the FairTax would fully untax any capital gains from the sales of used or new homes. It would also enable prospective home owners to save a down payment faster by increasing their take-home pay and not taxing their savings.

One more thing: as we've said, the FairTax is easy to attack, and its critics will surely try to tell Americans that the FairTax will "add 23 percent to the cost of every new home." We have quite a collection of letters from elected officials saying just that.

The same principles apply to new-home construction as apply to everything else you purchase in the retail marketplace. Every new home today carries an embedded tax: the combined tax burden of all the suppliers of materials and labor involved in the construction of that home. With the FairTax, that embedded burden would be removed and replaced by the FairTax.

The deeper message here is that many ideas about our tax code are based on long-held misunderstandings of how the tax code operates—misunderstandings so pervasive that they permeate even the highest levels of government. Bringing about a FairTax-size change would be hard enough if every one understood the lay of the land today—but we have much more work to do, starting with correcting all the misunderstandings that have been sold to the American people. Thank goodness we have a team of thousands!

Criticism: Ending the tax-deductible status of charitable contributions will destroy America's charitable organizations.

Some charities have expressed concern that their flow of contributions will dry up if the income tax advantage disappears. We've encountered this particular objection to the FairTax many times, and we're frankly at a loss as to how it makes any sense at all. The truth is that the incentive for giving to charitable organizations would not be diminished in any degree by the FairTax. In fact, it would increase.

Here's how. Under the current system, when you donate money to a qualified charity, you're permitted to deduct the amount you donated from your taxable income. Let's say your tax bracket is 25 percent and you donate $1,000. The charity gets the thousand bucks, and you get to lower your taxable income by the same amount. At a 25 percent tax rate, this means you lower your tax bill by $250.

Tell us, please: under what set of logical operating principles would a person give away $1,000 to save $250 in taxes? None. The happy truth is that people give their money to charities *because they feel charitable*. We've long since concluded that money is given less for tax reasons than for reasons of love and caring.

The more money people have in their pockets, the more of their paycheck they're allowed to keep, the more likely they are to give to charity, and the more money they're likely to give.

Your authors have seen this in their own lives. Our mothers never had an income in their lives that exceeded the poverty level. Yet they never failed to give to the church—or to the Girl Scouts. People give money away when they have money—any amount of money—in their pockets. And we're going to put more money in their pockets.

Americans' generous spirit runs very deep. We give more when we have more. In 1980, when the value of a contribution at the margin was 70 percent, we gave about $43 billion to charities. In 1988, when the value of a contribution at the margin was 28 percent, we gave $88 billion. The 1980s were good to Americans, and we simply had more to give in the latter part of the decade. Some of the nation's greatest fortunes—Andrew Carnegie's, John D. Rockefeller's, J. P. Morgan's—were given away when there was no tax deduction for charitable giving at all.

At the risk of overkill, here's even more evidence that the FairTax won't have an adverse effect on charitable giving: after the 1986 Tax Reform Act, charitable giving increased rather than decreased, despite the lowering of marginal income and transfer tax rates. Charitable giving rose by $6.4 billion, or 7.6 percent, in 1987, after the top tax rate fell from 50 percent to 28 percent, thus more than doubling the tax price of giving. Likewise, the growth of charitable bequests was most rapid from 1980 to 1987, when estate taxes were coming down.

According to *Giving USA 2004,* charitable contributions totaled $240.7 billion in 2003.[26] Of this amount, according to IRS data, 61 percent, or $145.7 billion, was claimed by the 30 percent of individual taxpayers who itemized deductions on their 2003 federal tax returns.[27] When the effect of the increase in income from the FairTax is combined with the effect of the change in the price of giving for both itemizers and nonitemizers, recent research by Beacon Hill Institute finds that charitable donations would increase by $2.06 billion. This translates to an almost 1 percent increase in the first year (2007), an increase of 2.4 percent within ten years of its introduction, and an increase of 5 percent after twenty years. These increases are in comparison to a baseline in which the current tax regime continues.[28]

---

26. American Association for Fundraising Council Trust for Philanthropy, *Giving USA 2004.*

27. Michael Parisi and Scott Hollenbeck, "Individual Tax Returns, 2003," IRS Statistics of Income. Available at www.irs.gov/pub/irs-soi/03indtr.pdf.

28. David G. Tuerck, Jonathan Haughton, Alfonso Sanchez-Penalver, Sara Dinwoodie, and Paul Bachman, "The FairTax and Charitable

So when do people increase their giving and when do they cut back? The key to these fluctuations is *the economy,* not the tax burden. Over the past forty years, the level of annual donations has tracked personal income growth almost exactly.[29] When the economy is up, along with personal income, Americans give. When the economy falls off a cliff, so does charitable giving. Americans are always generous, but the key to sustaining their giving is keeping the economy booming. Economists have consistently predicted a sustained boom in the American economy once consumption taxes replace income taxation.[30] This will drive charitable giving to new heights.

Giving," Beacon Hill Institute, February 2007; www.beaconhill.org/FairTax2007/FTaxCharitableGivingBHI4-24-07.pdf.

29. "The most overwhelming proof that tax incentives have a relatively minor effect on individual charity is the tremendous consistency over time of giving as a percentage of income. Although the tax code has changed frequently and dramatically over the past twenty-three years, giving as a share of personal income has hovered around 1.83 percent. This measure reached as high as 1.95 percent in 1989 and as low as 1.71 percent in 1985. The narrow range has persisted even though the top marginal tax rate has fluctuated in that period from between 28 and 70 percent. It suggests that raising income growth will do more to boost charitable giving than any tax incentive." John S. Barry, "Faith, Growth, and Charity," *Policy Review,* March 1997.

30. Look again at the Joint Tax Symposium discussed earlier.

Giving as a Percentage of GDP: 1973–2003

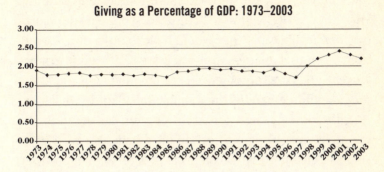

Source: Giving USA Annual Report 1996, *p. 56, updated with subsequent issues; and GDP data from the* Economic Report of the President, *February 1996, pp. 284, 308.*

So it's clear: charitable institutions have nothing to fear from the FairTax.

Criticism: The transition costs of moving to the FairTax would be unmanageable.

When discussing a significant change in the tax code—particularly when it involves throwing out the entire tax code and replacing with something new—serious people ask what will the transition costs be. It's a good question. But many of us believe the benefits outweigh the costs—no matter how high they may be.

The Retail Federation isn't what you might call fond of the FairTax. When they came calling, they argued that they would be forced to buy new point-of-sale registers to handle the change. We were stunned. Surely they were kidding! Were they really willing to scuttle such a great tax reform proposal just because they would have to buy new cash registers? For that matter, were they actually trying to convince us that the computerized cash registers in general use today couldn't handle the FairTax calculations? Let's get real: these new-generation cash registers can figure out a sale involving 10 percent off on all purchases over $39.99 and 15 percent off when the total gets to $99.99, but they can't figure out an inclusive 23 percent sales tax?

There are 85,525 units of local government in the U.S.[31] In the states that have a local or county sales tax, the rules change regularly. In Georgia we have a special-purpose local option sales tax (SPLOST), a device localities routinely use to collect funds for school construction or other infrastructure improvements. Is our local Target forced to run out and buy new registers every few months? Probably not. We're guessing it makes a programming adjustment and never misses a beat.

With that worry put to rest, let's look at the one transi-

---

31. U.S. Census Bureau, *Census of Governments, 2002*. From that report, "In addition to the federal government and the 50 state governments, there were 87,525 units of local government. Of these, 38,967 are general-purpose local governments—3,034 county governments, and 35,933 subcounty general-purpose governments (including 19,429 municipal governments and 16,504 town or township governments). The remainder, more than half the total number, are special-purpose local governments, including 13,506 school district governments and 35,052 special district governments."

tion rule in H.R. 25. Let's assume that the FairTax goes into effect on January 1, 2009. If a business has any inventory on hand as of December 31, 2008, a percentage of the value of that inventory can be used as a credit against the amount of tax due in the following year. That's because tax has already been embedded in the cost of that inventory along the line of its manufacturing, and we don't believe anything should be taxed twice. At any given time, there's roughly $2 trillion in inventory in America;[32] thus the amount of the inventory credit would be about $600 billion. Businesses would apply for the credit as their inventory is sold and have up to eighteen months to claim the credit.

Does that seem hideously expensive? Not from where we sit.

Remember, too, that $600 billion in embedded taxes in that inventory are taxes that have already been collected—so the cost of transition in terms of government revenue is actually *zero*!

Glenn Hubbard, a former economic adviser to President Bush, isn't a FairTax supporter. But even he told the House Ways and Means Committee that the transition would be uneventful. Alan Greenspan has said the same thing.

The very idea of a "transition cost" raises some interesting questions. Have you ever worried about a "sit-and-do-

---

32. U.S. Chamber of Commerce, Bureau of Economic Affairs, National Income Product Accounts, Table 5.7.5B, "Private Inventories and Domestic Final Sales by Industry"; www.bea.gov.

nothing cost" or an "avoid-taking-a-stand cost"? How about the "let the current tax code continue until it destroys America" cost? There may be some dislocations and hiccups as a result of the move to the FairTax—but compare those with the economic disaster that's coming if we keep our current system. Someone will definitely lose his or her job as a result of the move to the FairTax, but our market will be flooded with new jobs to replace it.

You can worry about transition costs; we're more concerned about "failure-to-transition costs": they might be too high for our nation to pay.

Criticism: This seems like a lot of trouble. Wouldn't a flat tax be easier?

Been there, done that, and all we got was this lousy tax code. Would a flat tax be easier? Probably. Would it be better? No way.

This flat-tax-versus-FairTax debate is one we love. No, not because we love a challenge. It's because we love easily winnable debates.

History lesson, folks: The tax system we have today—the one we've come to know and love—began ninety-four years ago as a (drum roll, please) *flat tax*! The monstrosity you see today is a flat tax on income after nearly a century of very imperfect evolution. At first, only a very small percentage of Americans were asked to pay income tax. In fact, that's how they sold it to us—as a tax on the rich!

Well, that all changed with World War II. The cost of

the war effort led to an expansion of those who paid federal income taxes—and we were off to the races. The tax code was flattened again, if you will, in 1986. Since that time it has been amended 16,000 times. We now have more than 67,000 pages of statutes and regulations—which helps explain why, last year, nearly two-thirds of all tax filers had to seek professional help with their tax return.

You must know that under the present system the chances of having an absolutely accurate tax return filed on your behalf are near zero. If you earn any significant income at all and you try to prepare your own tax return, your chances of preparing one that is error-free are less than zero. Better you should try to win the lottery. Then again, if you call the IRS help line, your chances of getting a correct answer are less than 60 percent.

Where does all of this leave us? With a tax code that's wholly inefficient in raising the necessary monies to fund the government (and that's putting it kindly). And it gives us a code that politicians love to use to tell you how to live your life.

Remember, a flat tax is nowhere near as comprehensive a solution to our problems as the FairTax. Under a flat tax, we'd still be facing payroll tax deductions. You'd still have to report your income. And the IRS would still be there to pry into your personal financial affairs.

There's a reason that one of the principal proponents of the flat tax once told Congressman Linder, "I like your idea better." This individual is now wed to a tax reform proposal he knows is second rate. When we went looking for the best tax reform proposal, we knew it when we saw it—the FairTax.

Criticism: If we must have a consumption tax, a value-added tax (VAT) would be better.

The value-added tax has been the most common choice among nations that have moved to a consumption tax model. It's a tax on each step of the manufacturing process in which a business buys a product and adds value to it. For example, in the making of an automobile, an ore company buys equipment and hires workers to get ore out of the ground to sell to a steel manufacturer. The manufacturer deducts the cost it incurs from the sale price and pays a tax on the difference. The steel company sells the steel to a company that shapes bumpers and pays tax on the value of the sale minus their costs. And on it goes: at each step along the way a small tax is imposed on the increased value.

It's true that the tax on the increase in value is very small at each step along the supply chain. But all those taxes accumulate along the way. By the time the consumer buys the product for final consumption, the total cost of the tax burden is hidden in that final price, to be paid by the final consumer.

Many economists argue that the VAT is preferable to a sales tax because the costs of administering it are lower and compliance is better. That is true.

In the income tax paradigm the taxes taken from your paycheck and collected by your employer are remitted to the federal government and have a very high rate of collection. VAT advocates argue that corporations would collect a value-added tax more efficiently and more accurately than retailers would collect the FairTax.

In response to our claim that the FairTax sends goods and services into a global economy with no tax component in the price system, they point out that the VAT levied by European companies, for example, is generally rebated to the companies when the product is exported, so that the product goes abroad with no tax component in its price.

All of the above arguments are true, and all inure to the benefit of the government.

But what about private-sector businesses? Again, there is the issue of compliance costs. Under the FairTax, businesses will encounter compliance costs only when they're dealing with customers at the retail level. Even then, retail providers would get to keep a small portion of the collected FairTax to cover those costs. With the VAT, businesses throughout the chain of production have to do the paperwork necessary to deduct cost from price. Why go through the extra trouble when there's a better plan on the table?

Our concern is more practical. We follow Milton Friedman's observation that "the VAT is the most efficient way to raise taxes and the most effective way to increase the size of the government."

Since the VAT is levied at so many steps along the manufacturing chain, a very small increase raises a significant amount of revenue; the average consumer thinks this is just a matter of inflation.

Europe, whose member nations levy a VAT, taxes its citizens at about 40 to 45 percent of its entire economy. It has seen virtually no increase in jobs for twenty-five years. The exception is Ireland. Why? Because Ireland reduced the tax burden on its citizens, a move that transformed the small nation into Europe's fastest-growing economy.

There's one more very important danger associated with the VAT: many countries that use this system *also* have an income tax. Is that what we want in the United States? One year we may be singing the praises of a VAT. A few years later, Americans could find themselves with a VAT *on top of* an income tax.

We tax our citizens at about 25 percent of the economy. We believe we can reduce that burden by moving to a simpler, fairer tax system—and that *you,* who will see the cost of your government every time you buy a loaf of bread, will force a reduction in the tax.

One more thing: can someone tell us how the VAT untaxes the poor?

Criticism: If we abolish the high income tax rates paid by the wealthy—and completely exempt the poor—won't the middle class end up footing the bill?

The answer to this question is definite and twofold. First, if you're a middle-class American living beyond your means today, you'll definitely pay more under the FairTax than you do now—and that may not be a bad thing, because living beyond your means isn't something to be proud of.

Unfortunately, today's income tax subsidizes debt and penalizes savings, so it's no wonder that many people choose a debt-filled path.

Second, you'd be absolutely right about the middle class getting squeezed *if* we were to repeal only the income tax. In fact, when the President's Advisory Panel on Federal Tax Reform examined and rejected a sales tax to replace the income tax, it did so for exactly that reason. The FairTax, however, proposes to repeal *both* the income tax and the payroll tax—and that payroll tax part makes all the difference, because that's the largest tax working Americans pay . . . and wealthy Americans generally don't pay a dime of it.

Let's look at this in more detail.

Before the income tax was instituted, the U.S. government was funded largely by tariffs and excise taxes. After 1913 we began to tax wages. The income tax and payroll tax are levied on how much money you earn in wages.

Today, the average taxpayer is in the 25 percent tax bracket and pays an additional 7.65 percent (we can round this number up to 8 percent for easy math) for the employee's share of the payroll tax that pays for Social Security and Medicare. The Social Security portion of the payroll tax is applied against the first $97,500 of wages. The Medicare tax is levied on all wages, with no cap.

Income from wealth, however, has always been taxed differently. Today, the tax on capital gains and dividends is 15 percent. That has varied over the years, but since the 1986 tax reform that tax has been less than the tax on income at the highest levels. In addition, no payroll tax is levied against capital gains or dividends. This lower rate is good for the country, mind you—the capital gains rate, especially, encourages investment, which is what is needed to create jobs.

When we lower the tax rate on capital gains and dividends, we see huge increases in revenues from those sources for two reasons. First, a high capital gains tax rate causes investors to hold on to their investments, to avoid the high tax penalty. Second, a low tax rate on dividends encourages corporations to start paying dividends (or increase them), thus yielding more revenues to the government. This shows once again that lower tax rates are good for the economy.

Now comes the important part: The first thing very wealthy people do when money starts pouring in is to stop getting a wage. They live on their capital gains and dividends and pay a 15 percent tax rate. They pay nothing to Social Security and Medicare because they have no wages.

The FairTax taxes spending instead of wages. We would all pay the FairTax—which would fund Social Security and Medicare in addition to general government—on 100 percent of our spending (beyond poverty-level spending for our household size).

The question is, would you rather pay the government a marginal rate of 33 percent of what you earn or 23 percent of what you spend? How can the rate be lower and still collect the same amount of income? Because the FairTax consumption base has no special exceptions or exemptions; it's simply that much larger than the current income tax base, which is riddled with loopholes and special treatment.

One more thing to consider as we discuss the effect of the FairTax on the middle class: The latest Treasury statistics show a great deal of mobility, generally upward, in lower- and middle-income levels. Today's middle income earners aspire to be in the upper income levels in subsequent years, and with a bit of hard work and good decision skills, this is how things generally work out. While certain middle-income earners with a high debt-to-income ratio might feel a bit of a bite from the FairTax, the economic growth brought about by the FairTax would quickly propel them into higher-income levels, where they'd no longer feel that bite. The FairTax rewards those who live responsibly at all income levels—and what's that we keep saying about getting more of the behavior you reward?

Criticism: The progressive nature of our current tax code is important to me, and the FairTax will eliminate it.

Still thinking of attacking the FairTax as less "progressive" than our current system? We hope not, because we thought we covered a bit of that in our "middle-class" section above. But there's definitely more to say on the subject. Only time will tell, but the truth is that the FairTax could be even more progressive than our current system. Here's why.

- It repeals payroll taxes, which account for 38 percent of all federal taxes and fall disproportionately

on low- and middle-income wage earners. The regressive payroll tax burdens wages (not dividends,
interest, or capital gains) up to $97,500 at 15.3 per-
cent.

- It entirely untaxes the poor and reduces the tax
  burden on the near poor by exempting all consumption up to the poverty line, giving each family a tax-
  free consumption allowance.

- It saves more than 80 percent of the $400 billion–
  plus in compliance costs—yet another hidden tax
  borne disproportionately by the poor and middle
  class.[33]

- It fosters economic growth, which will increase real
  wages—which will benefit the poor and middle
  class.

Of course, as we all know, whether a tax system is "fair"
is a complicated economic and philosophical question, one
that inevitably involves oversimplification and subjective
judgment. For our purposes, the real concern is whether
taxpayers will have more money in their pockets after the
switch to the FairTax than before.

If you look at this question from different angles, what
you find may surprise you. First, let's examine what effect

---

33. A Tax Foundation study for 2002 has found that taxpayers with
adjusted gross incomes under $20,000 incur a compliance cost of
4.53 percent of income compared to only 0.29 percent for taxpayers
with adjusted gross incomes over $200,000.

the FairTax will have on the tax rates of low-, middle-, and high-income folks. (This section will draw on some of the top-notch economic research that went into developing the FairTax in the first place, much of it done by Boston University's Larry Kotlikoff, so it may get a little technical at times. Those who want even more econospeak are free to dip into the footnotes.)

The research shows that the FairTax will significantly reduce the tax rate on work and savings, thereby substantially lowering the overall tax burdens on current and future workers.[34] Today, marginal tax rates (the amount of tax on the next dollar earned or saved) are higher—in some cases much higher—for almost all American households than they would be under a revenue-neutral FairTax. The current system's tax rate on wages exceeds the FairTax's 23 percent rate for nine out of ten of the household types in the study. For some low- and middle-income households, the tax incurred working under our current tax system was more than twice the 23 percent FairTax rate. Why? Because some low-income couples with children who receive the

---

34. Kotlikoff bases this conclusion on a detailed model computing the tax burdens for 42 different household types: seven different income groupings; and both singles and couples, ages 30, 45, and 60. Laurence Kotlikoff and David Rapson, "Comparing Average and Marginal Tax Rates under the FairTax and the Current System of Federal Taxation," October 2006. Available at http://people.bu.edu/kotlikoff/Comparing%20Average%20and%20Marginal%20Tax%20Rates%2010-17-06.pdf.

Earned Income Tax Credit face a tax of almost fifty cents on the next dollar earned as the EITC phases out.

The FairTax encourages savings with a zero tax rate on savings. This is in stark contrast to the existing tax code, which imposes very high tax rates on saving, ranging from 23 to 54 percent, depending on whether the taxpayer is a single person or a married couple. While the rate structure of the current tax code encourages consumption, the FairTax taxes current and future consumption at the same rate—which ends the savings penalty and allows citizens a fair opportunity to save for the future.

The future? That's right. Save for the future, and good things will happen. We know this intuitively, and this principle is incorporated into the economics behind the FairTax. To get the full picture, we need to look beyond the "How will I be treated this year?" charts tax writers in Washington have long promoted. Instead, let's look at how the FairTax will affect you over your lifetime.

Do you think solely in the short term, or is the long term important to you as well?

As any economist would expect, we have good news: the FairTax lifetime tax burden would be lower for all household types than under the current system. That's right. Because of the growth, savings, and investment potential inherent in the system, in the course of a lifetime everyone wins under the FairTax—single and married households, young and old, and low- and high-earning households. Without exception, one recent study confirmed, all household types would have lower average lifetime tax rates under the FairTax than under the current system.[35]

To determine whether this new tax system would leave people better off than they were, we must look into the future, to compare where we'll be if the current system remains in place against the future in a FairTax world. Will there be short-term dislocations? Absolutely. Will you owe more in taxes in the first year of a FairTax system than you do today? As discussed, depending on your spending behavior, you might.

But what happens if the current system remains in place? Well, how'd you like to see your payroll taxes double? That's right: more than a doubling of the payroll tax rate will be necessary to fund Social Security. Thank today's wizened citizens for living so long. These increased Social Security taxes will lead to a 21 percent decline in future after-tax take-home pay. Remember who pays the payroll tax? That's right: wage earners. This giant tax increase—which under the current system can be avoided by only cutting benefits—will result in a major reduction in economic well-being, which can be avoided by switching to the FairTax.[36]

---

35. The calculation of the average remaining lifetime tax rates takes into account total taxes paid over one's remaining lifetime minus Social Security benefits and the FairTax prebate. This figure is divided by total lifetime income to get the lifetime tax rate.

36. Laurence J. Kotlikoff and Sabine Jokisch, "Simulating the Dynamic Macroeconomic and Microeconomic Effects of the FairTax,"

What does a FairTax future look like? Switching to the FairTax would dramatically increase investment in plant and equipment. Indeed, American capital stock would almost double by 2100. This increased investment would lead to higher productivity, which in turn would increase real wages per unit of labor. Rather than declining by 8 percent by the end of the century, as it will under the current system, the real wage would now rise by 17 percent—a 25 percent difference in workers' real compensation. The pace of the change may be slow, but by 2030 real wages under the FairTax would be 11.5 percent higher than they would be if the current system remains in place. In transforming the economy's prospect from one of a capital shortage to one of capital deepening, the FairTax would also reduce real interest rates.[37] What home-buying, car-purchasing, credit card–maxing American wouldn't be grateful for that? Interest rate reductions are the gift that keeps on giving, payment after monthly payment.

"Sure," you say. "Of course the FairTax will be good for the young folks. They'll get all of its long-term economic benefits, plus they'll be saved from the crushing burden of paying for me, the hypothetical older American. But what is in it for me?" Honestly, we don't think most grandpar-

---

National Tax Journal, June 1, 2007; http://people.bu.edu/kotlikoff/FairTax%20NTJ%20Final%20Version,%20April%2024,%202007.pdf.
37. Ibid., Table 4.

ents take that view. The World War II generation has always looked out for the welfare of others, and we think that their vote on the FairTax will be no exception.

Just in case we're wrong, though, let's see what would happen for them.

We'll start with the results of the Kotlikoff study for those born in 1920. The low-income members of this age group would experience a sizable 9.4 percent increase in their economic well-being. (The economic term of art for this increase is "welfare gain," but "welfare" has so many negative connotations—particularly when we're talking about government and taxes—that we prefer to avoid it.) Their middle-income contemporaries would experience a moderate 1.0 percent economic improvement, while their richer contemporaries would sustain a small, 0.4 percent welfare loss. This picture of substantial gains for low-income group members, and modest gains or slight losses for middle- and high-income cohort members, holds for all age groups born before 1970. People born after 1970, on the other hand, will see major improvements in their economic well-being—not just for low-income cohort members but for middle- and high-income members as well. Take the age group born in 2030: low-income members would experience a 26.3 percent gain, while their middle-income contemporaries would experience a 12.4 percent gain and their high-income contemporaries would experience a 5.0 percent gain.

Over the long haul, the FairTax offers a real opportunity to improve the U.S. economy's performance and the well-being of the vast majority of Americans. To begin with, it cuts in half the long-term increase in the effective rate of wage taxation needed to pay the Social Security and health care benefits of an aging country. The improvement in the economy has important implications for the economic well-being of individuals as well. Low-income households would experience a 26.7 percent welfare gain, middle-income households would experience a 10.9 percent welfare gain, and high-income households would experience a 4.7 percent welfare gain. This is a very progressive long-term outcome. But progressivity marks the entire transition. Existing low-income households, whether they are young, middle-aged, or old, would all experience welfare gains ranging from 4.7 percent to more than 20 percent.[38]

In sum, as it changes our approach from taxing income

---

38. See ibid., Table 5. If you're up for it, here is why Americans would see these big gains. Thanks to the FairTax, they would receive a pretax wage at the start of their work careers (roughly midcentury) that would be 19.6 percent higher than it would otherwise have been. By the end of their work careers, their pretax wage would be 25.0 percent higher than it would otherwise have been. In addition, they would receive the FairTax prebate. Hence, these households would pay relatively little in taxes, net, and face an average net tax on their labor earnings of only 5 percent. In contrast, their average net tax under the status quo regime ranges from 19.5 percent to 23.6 percent over the course of their work span, due to their exposure to payroll (FICA) taxation. Finally, these households would

to taxing consumption and adding a highly progressive prebate, the FairTax introduces many progressive elements into our fiscal system, removes one very regressive element (the payroll tax), and provides much better incentives to work and save. It also generates major welfare gains for the poorest members of society, including those now retired and those yet to be born.

The economist Larry Kotlikoff captures our sentiments exactly: "[M]y preferred reform is the FairTax, which has three highly progressive elements. First, thanks to the [p]rebate, poor households would pay no sales taxes in net terms. Second, the reform eliminates our highly regressive FICA tax. Third, the sales tax will effectively tax wealth as well as wages: When the rich spend their wealth and when workers spend their wages, they will both pay sales taxes. By broadening the effective tax base to include the corpus of wealth, not just the income earned on it (much of which is currently exempted or taxed at a low rate), one can lower the required sales tax rate and, thereby, reduce the tax burden on workers."[39]

---

experience substantial efficiency gains thanks to the FairTax's complete elimination of the taxation of saving.

39. Laurence J. Kotlikoff, "Averting America's Bankruptcy with a New, New Deal," *The Economists' Voice*, February 2006, revised March 13, 2007. Available at http://people.bu.edu/kotlikoff/New%20New%20Deal%203-13-071.pdf.

Change in Economic Well-Being under the FairTax
(by income class and birth year)

Are you still worried that we're not punishing the rich enough? For those who believe that the rich should be punished with an even greater than 23 percent tax on their spending, we have a few words of warning: economic theory and empirical research demonstrate that attempts to target the wealthy with higher marginal rates have their own negative consequences.

First, the highest income groups have the wherewithal to arrange their finances to avoid the tax, and the surtax on the wealthy creates only the appearance that they are paying at a higher rate. Tax planning is a lucrative profession because the professionals are successful at what they are doing. Throw more high rates at them, and we'll only be creating more tax planners, not more federal revenue.

Second, targeting these individuals would inevitably have negative effects on low- and middle-income groups. As the economist Michael Schuyler has pointed out:

When a tax on upper-income individuals causes them to work and save less, part of the tax burden is shifted to the rest of the population, including lower-income individuals. As high-productivity, upper-income people cut the time and intensity of their work effort due to a higher tax rate on their labor effort, they employ fewer people to work with them, and their reduced presence in the workplace lowers the productivity and incomes of other workers.

As upper-income individuals save and invest less due to a higher tax rate on their capital income (the higher tax rate can be at the corporate level, the shareholder level, or on income from non-corporate businesses), capital formation drops, which reduces the amounts of plant, equipment, buildings, and other structures. The smaller capital stock decreases the productivity of labor, thereby reducing jobs and wages. Because of these tax-induced effects, middle- and lower-income workers indirectly bear a significant part of the burden of the taxes on higher-income individuals. Middle- and lower-income earners also suffer from a lower stock market if they own shares directly or through pension funds. Middle- and lower-income workers additionally bear some of the tax as consumers, because output is reduced, and consumers of all income levels must make do with fewer, higher priced goods and services.[40]

40. Michael Schuyler, "A Miserable Tax (The AMT) May Become Worse," Institute for Research on the Economics of Taxation, *IRET Congressional Advisory,* May 30, 2007.

Whew. That was exhausting. Look—if you're going to develop a completely new tax system for America and then write a book that addresses criticisms of that plan in a comprehensive manner, you've got to expect to handle some difficult language somewhere along the way. Time to move on.

Criticism: I've been saving all my life. I paid taxes on all of that money I put in my savings accounts. Now you want to tax me again when I spend that money. That's not fair.

By now the response to this criticism should be self-evident, but we'll address it here just so nobody will accuse us of ignoring it.

Yes, you've been saving all your life. And, yes, you've already paid income taxes on that money you put into your savings or investment account. And, yes again, under the FairTax you're going to be taxed when you take that money out of your savings account and spend it.

So what else is new?

Think for a moment. You're going to be taxed *anyway*! When you take that money out of your savings or investment account and spend it, either you're going to pay the embedded taxes that lurk in every product and service you consume, or you're going to pay the FairTax. Six of one, half-dozen of the other. However—and here's your bonus— under the FairTax you're going to be receiving the prebate. Everything you buy with those savings is going to cost pretty much the same—plus you'll have that prebate check every month. Still sound like a bad deal?

Criticism: It's not going to happen.

This criticism is particularly vexing. These people aren't saying that the FairTax isn't a good idea. They're not saying it won't work. They're not saying that the research is flawed or that the FairTax is being misrepresented to the people. They just say, "It's a good idea, but it isn't going to happen."

Let's hop into the way-back machine to see if we can find any other times in the history of our country when people were saying "It just isn't going to happen."

Let's set the dials to 1776. George Washington and his ragtag army are fighting for our country's independence from Great Britain. Many modern readers may be surprised to learn this, but at no time during our Revolutionary War did the majority of colonists support the idea of independence. From 1776 until victory in 1783, it was the minority who either fought for independence or supported those who did.

What about the majority? They were sitting back and clucking, "It's not going to happen."

Is this what remains of the American spirit today? Millions of dollars are spent and hundreds of thousands of volunteers line up to develop and promote a tax reform plan that could well turn the tide, both economically and politically, in our country—and we just walk away, muttering "Never gonna happen"? New England is full of two-hundred-year-old headstones marking the graves of people who, instead of saying "It isn't going to happen," said "This can happen, but only if I get behind it and do my part."

How sad it would be if the FairTax came so very close to reality, then failed legislatively because a few people—people who could really have helped, people who could have made such a positive difference—just shrugged their shoulders and said "Hey, it's a good idea, but I don't see it happening."

As the Reverend Robert Schuller is fond of saying, "If it's going to be, it's up to me." Basketball players have taken to repeating the phrase in their practice drills while passing the ball around. "If it's going to be, it's up to me" is a mantra repeated by doers—people who are driven to succeed.

The FairTax, as we've said, would be the most massive transfer of power from the government to the people in the history of our country. It is, in every respect, a twenty-first-century American revolution. Thankfully, for every person who would dismiss it with "Not going to happen," there are dozens more who are willing to dedicate their time, energy, and even money to an effort to see that it does.

There very well may be some other good criticisms that we've missed. It isn't intentional. We're not dodging anyone. But even if we did miss one, we hope we've given you enough grounding to handle those criticisms on your own.

If you find yourself confronting a critique we haven't addressed, first consider whether the criticism really has to do with the substance or principles of the FairTax. If not ("I don't like the name FairTax—who gets to say what fair is, anyway?") you can safely dismiss it. Save your energy for more important questions about fundamental tax reform.

If the criticism does address one of the principles ("The FairTax is too complicated for taxpayers to understand"), try looking more closely. Is it really a criticism of the Fair-Tax vision or of its expression in H.R. 25? If the latter, you're welcome to give it some thought—and if you come up with some ideas about how to improve the language of the FairTax bill, feel free to send your suggestions to us or the folks at FairTax.org.

If the criticism you're wrestling is a more substantial matter ("Taxes should be easy to pay and collect, but the FairTax isn't"), take things one step further. In some cases, you may find that the critic is simply mistaken about the particulars of the FairTax; often a simple explanation will put the criticism to rest. In other cases, the criticisms may be valid; they may point to some less-than-desirable effects the FairTax may bring about, in the short or long term ("The prebate system is necessary to protect the poor, but it'll be subject to fraud and abuse—frustrating the goal of efficient collection and enforcement"). In this case, it's up to you to sit down and decide whether those ill effects would be important enough to scuttle the whole FairTax idea.

As we've said before, if this were easy, we'd be done already. But with a volunteer base of hundreds of thousands of thoughtful taxpayers applying themselves to these questions and helping us with these answers, we're confident that—criticisms and all—the FairTax is the best opportunity for tax reform and economic growth this country has ever seen.

11

THE FAIRTAX GRASSROOTS ARMY–AND ITS VICTORIES

If anyone tells you that all you need to do is cast your vote in November and we can make the FairTax a reality, he's leading you astray. Casting your vote for a candidate for economic change and growth is a good first step, but implementing the principles of the FairTax is going to require more. We hope this book has convinced you to be a part of that process, if you aren't already. And if you already are—if you're part of the "If it's going to be, it's up to me" crowd, not the "It's not going to happen" crowd—we want to take a few pages to brag about you!

In 2007, your coauthors Linder and Boortz went to Ames, Iowa, for the "straw poll."

Clearly Mitt Romney had the biggest presence. It's been estimated that he spent $3 million to $5 million to get there, renting buses to bring in supporters from each of Iowa's ninety counties. In polling running up to the event, he was the clear leader. Rudy Giuliani and John McCain chose not to participate. Fred Thompson was not yet a declared candidate.

Who stole the show? Americans for Fair Taxation, that's who. There were FairTax volunteers all over the grounds. You couldn't walk ten feet without bumping into someone with a FairTax sticker on his or her shirt, a FairTax hat, or a sign.

Romney, an opponent of the FairTax, had his supporters wearing yellow T-shirts. About a third of them had a FairTax sticker on their shirt. When the votes were cast, Romney was the winner, with 31 percent. Former Arkansas Governor Mike Huckabee, who spent less than $150,000, came in second, with 18 percent of the vote.

How did he do that? Simple: he ran on the FairTax.

After the caucus, Huckabee told us something interesting. All the candidates have been asked in debates whether they would sign the FairTax if it were passed by Congress. Huckabee responded by calling that the wrong question. "The president won't have a chance to sign it unless he is willing to sell it. I'm willing to sell it."

This is going to be an important issue in the presidential election, perhaps the most important of the past thirty years. This election can alter the course of this country's history. FairTax advocates have no inclination to let the candidates rest during this campaign season. Every candidate will be asked at every stop whether he or she supports the FairTax.

In fact, every member of Congress confronts questions about the FairTax at every public event. That is what the thousands of volunteers are bringing to this debate on a daily basis, and we cannot thank them enough. When Dan Boren, a Democrat from Oklahoma, signed on, he told us that the FairTax was everywhere in his district.

From the beginning of the research to the introduction of H.R. 25, we knew there was no way to convince enough politicians that we should throw out the tax code for a new idea. With roughly half of all the lobbyists in Washington making a living off gaming the current code, we knew we'd never get enough support to start the groundswell in that town. Instead, we concluded, the idea must move the nation first—and then the nation would move Congress.

That seems to be happening, and not just in Ames, Iowa. The million-plus people who have signed petitions of support for the FairTax are talking about it every day. The proponents who respond to the negative articles, with thoughtful and respectful responses, are educating the nation. The 300,000 volunteers who have offered their time will help swamp Washington with phone calls, e-mails, and letters.

This is all great—but it's not enough. We need to do more. It's likely that less than 40 percent of the nation has heard of the FairTax. It's just as likely that half of Congress has no real idea of exactly how it would work.[1]

If you're inclined to get involved, contact FairTax.org and sign up. If you want to be a "citizen cosponsor" of the FairTax, go to JohnLinder.com and sign up. You'll get updates and instructions for action.

Finally—and this is important—members of Congress hear from lobbyists all the time, but the requests they really respond to come from their constituents. Obviously, with thousands of FairTax advocates across the country, there's no way we can mention everyone who has made an impact on the FairTax's success, but we're not going to let that stop us from trying to recognize a few. The FairTax effort is nothing without men and women like you participating in it, advocating for it, and voting based upon it—so we want to cite and thank as many as we can. Your state has leaders just as strong as these—track them down and ask them how you can help!

Gene Key in Georgia leads that state's FairTax organization. Last year he organized five workshops in Georgia and another in Alabama, where interested individuals showed

---

1. Most members of Congress rely on aides to brief them on bills and policy matters such as the FairTax. Those aides have a vested interest in keeping their jobs. A tax aide to an elected official might well be reluctant to give that official an honest appraisal of the Fair-Tax. With tax reform of this type, aides' jobs might quickly become unnecessary. It's so much easier just to tell the boss something like "It's not a good plan, sir. It would add 30 percent to the cost of everything people buy."

up for a three-hour informational meeting. He typically has about a hundred people show up to learn about the Fair-Tax—people who then take what they learn and share it in churches, civic groups, and businesses. Angela Bean in Georgia typically leads those meetings, answering questions about the bill from newcomers and veterans alike. She very likely knows as much about the FairTax as we do.

Lori Klein in Arizona has spoken on scores of radio talk shows and crisscrossed the nation in support of the FairTax. She has helped raised funds for the national campaign and has worked closely with FairTax.org to bring elected officials to the cause. Lori can be found at almost every FairTax event, hosting training sessions for local volunteers and asking anyone who will listen to help buy radio and print ads for the FairTax and to help build the citizen army necessary to win the issue.

Marilyn Rickert in Oak Forest, Illinois, discovered the FairTax at the same time she discovered the Internet—while healing from a broken leg in 1996. She was skeptical at first, but the more she learned the more she believed, and now she's an active and dynamic citizen voice for the FairTax. She organizes, writes, and talks to everyone she can to advance the cause.

Phil Hinson in Georgia has traveled far and wide to support the FairTax for years. More people have heard Phil speak on the FairTax than almost any other speaker. He's been invited to speak to groups wanting to learn more about the FairTax throughout the Southeast, and he brings his passion to his own FairTax radio show in Atlanta. A thoughtful student of the FairTax and its promise for America, Phil often posts his insights on the Internet as podcasts.

Roger Buckholtz in Kalamazoo, Michigan, has led an effort to develop a statewide FairTax organization, complete with media spokespeople. He makes frequent appearances on radio shows and leads grassroots organizing by congressional district. Michigan is now considering a FairTax system at the state level largely because of Roger's work.

When Bill Spillane in California first heard about the FairTax on a radio ad in 1997, he knew that his previous work to eliminate the corporate income tax—recognized by President Ronald Reagan—had been "child's play" (in his words) compared to the beneficial effects of the FairTax. A former fighter jock and commercial airline pilot, Bill believes strongly that the "Made in America" label will come roaring back to life with the passage of the FairTax, and he works tirelessly to advance the cause.

John Collett in Kansas has worked all over the Midwest for years to bring the FairTax message to American farmers. He has led the effort to bring along the American Farm Bureau, going from county to county to explain the advantages to farmers of eliminating the inheritance tax, eliminating embedded taxes from the cost of farm equipment prices, and putting American commodities on a level playing field with foreign crops sold here and abroad.

Dan Mastromarco and David Burton in Virginia have been bringing their economic and legal expertise to the FairTax since its inception, putting the FairTax ideas into legislative language and then explaining that language throughout the nation's capital. You'll find their passionate FairTax papers and critical responses throughout the FairTax .org Web site and other think-tank sites, as well as in testimony for Congress's tax-writing committees.

Mark Gupton of Jacksonville, Florida, first read *The Fair-Tax Book* on a flight from Jacksonville to Seattle in September 2005. He was so intrigued that he read it again on the return flight and a third time at home. He was hooked on the best thing that could happen to America and has been a strong voice for the FairTax ever since. He has helped organize thirteen FairTax groups in Florida. Mark's mantra says it best: "Organize, organize, organize."

Al Ose loved the flat tax until he learned about the FairTax. "It's just the right thing to do," he tells anyone who will listen in his role as regional director of FairTax.org for Wisconsin and Iowa. Al has seen hundreds of his letters to the editor printed, has given scores of speeches, and has appeared on radio and television programs since 1998 in support of the FairTax. Al even wrote his own book: *America's Best Kept Secret: The FairTax.*

Billy Harrington, Robert Semands, and Carol Chouinard have been at work in Oklahoma. All but one federal legislator in Oklahoma have become cosponsors of the Fair-Tax legislation because of the work of these three great local leaders and others in the state. Robert Semands has worked from day one to interest others, including FairTax.org State Director and retired Marine Billy Harrington. Billy has one word of advice when it comes to organizing district directors and attending Town Hall meetings: "persistence." Carol Chouinard has worked from the local precinct level on up to see the FairTax become party policy. All three are working hard with other Oklahoma FairTaxers to convince officials there that the FairTax would work well at the state level as well.

And last, but definitely not least, we want to recognize those of you who have written letters to the editors of your local newspapers across the nation. You all deserve a very special mention for the impact you've had. Though your faces are unknown to us, your words and passion are bringing the FairTax closer to reality. Brad Hill wrote to the *Lancaster Eagle Gazette* in Ohio to explain the benefits of the FairTax for small business people. Hugh Williams wrote to the *Omaha World-Herald* to explain the fairness of the FairTax to Nebraskans. In Arizona, Marni Spletter's letter was published under the headline "FairTax would benefit workers" in the *Tucson Citizen*. In Kansas, Charles Cusic's FairTax passion led the Opinion page in the *Topeka Capital-Journal*. In Virginia, Timothy Dobbins defended the FairTax against detractors in the pages of the *Roanoke Times*. Under the heading "FairTax Facts Outweigh Myths," Anthony Fulmer defended the FairTax to Georgia and South Carolina readers in *The Augusta Chronicle*. Tony Atkins shared the FairTax with readers of the *Chicago Daily Herald*, and Martin White did the same thing in the *Knoxville News-Sentinel*. These are only a handful of the grassroots activists who have defended and promoted the FairTax. The fact that the FairTax can't be ignored anywhere in the nation because of letter writers like these brings us one giant step closer to making the FairTax a reality.

The list goes on: we'd mention plenty more names if our publisher would only spring for the paper. If you demand a *FairTax: Volume 3,* we'll pick up where we left off. But our real point is that the FairTax isn't just AFFT, and it definitely isn't just us. It's the collective effort of millions— and it is vibrant and alive. A movement this large can never stay alive on the backs of a small team. It must be buoyed by individuals who feel called to dedicate their time and re- sources to it. The FairTax is just such a phenomenon, and we're grateful to all who participate.

12

OUR VISION FOR TOMORROW

You've read *The FairTax Book* (at least we hope you have), and now you're at the end of *FairTax: The Truth*. With luck, you're convinced. If you are, we're glad.

If you're not . . . Well, tell us, what can we do? Would a personal visit help? Do you want us to come take you out for dinner? What is it going to take?

Look, we've handled pretty much every substantial objection that's ever been thrown at the FairTax. We even took the time to respond to that Scientology nonsense. Of course, that doesn't mean we've dealt with every single objection—just the ones that seem relatively well thought out and have been presented with some degree of earnest-ness. We more or less ignored, for instance, the claim that we're interested in the FairTax only because we're "rich"[1] and we want to get out of paying income taxes. (All right, we mentioned it once. Got under our skin.) We could spend more time trying to explain the difference between taxing wealth and taxing income, but what good would that do? Besides, we're both close enough to retirement[2] that soon we won't have any income to tax anyway.

No, we'd much rather spend our time on one last effort to convince you to climb aboard the FairTax bandwagon—to put aside all but the most basic life-sustaining functions and become a volunteer for the FairTax.

We're going to ask you to crank up your imagination for a moment here—and by *you*, we mean those of you who think this FairTax thing is a bad idea. Drop all your precon-ceptions for just a moment while we paint a little scenario for you to consider.

We want you to try to picture life under the FairTax. Just imagine: for your entire life you've been living and working in a United States where the federal government is funded by the FairTax, not a tax on your income. For the moment, forget all your misgivings about whether the Fair-Tax will really work. Just sit back and let us tell you how your day-to-day life would be under the FairTax.

---

1. One of us sort of is, one of us kind of isn't.
2. One of us is, one of us can't make up his mind.

Here would be the basic economic framework of your life under the FairTax:

- Every payday, you've been getting your complete paycheck. No deductions. No withholding for income tax, Social Security tax, Medicare tax. If you earn $2,000 per week, you get a check for $4,000 every two weeks. There will be no distinction between what you earn and your "take-home pay."
- Throughout your work life, whenever you earn a raise or changed jobs for more pay, you'll never have to try to figure out how much of that raise or how much of your new paycheck you'll be able to "keep." A $5,200-a-year raise will always mean an extra $200 in your paycheck every other week.
- You'll never had to save receipts or create any records pertaining to federal taxes. The only receipt you'll need to keep is the one for that ugly dress your husband bought for you, so you can return it when he's not looking.
- You'll always be able to invest what you earn without first having to pay any federal taxes on it. Every time you have money left over at the end of the month, you'll be able to put that money into a savings account or other investment. That money will never be taxed; nor will the interest you earn or the gains on your investment.
- When your parents die, they will leave you everything they have, just as their parents did for them—

no taxes due. And you know you'll be able to leave whatever you have earned and accumulated to whomever you wish[3] without any tax consequences. You'll never know the death of a loved one to be a taxable event.

- Every time you go to the store to buy an item and the price tag reads $19.99, you hand a $20 bill to the cashier and receive one penny as change. All your life, the price tag on the item will be the price you pay at the cash register. The tax man will take his 23 percent out of that purchase price. The only annoying thing about this whole affair is that stupid little trick of trying to make something seem cheaper by lopping one cent off the price.

- There are four people in your household: you, your spouse, and two rug rats. At the beginning of every month you've been getting a credit to your checking or savings account in the amount of $506 to compensate you for the federal sales taxes that are included in the price of everything you were expecting to buy during that month—right up to the poverty level. This has ensured that you're always able to purchase the basic necessities for your family without paying any tax whatsoever to the federal government.

- For you, paying taxes to the federal government will always be voluntary. You saved your money after providing the basics to your family, and you won't

3. The authors of this book would be a good start.

be taxed. You spent your money, you paid your taxes: your choice.

- You'll never have to fill out a federal tax return.
- You'll never receive a letter from the IRS.
- For all you know, IRS agents work for the Iowa Railroad System.
- Your bank will never make a report to the federal government on your deposit or withdrawal habits, either with or without your knowledge.
- The federal government will never surreptitiously go to your bank to poke through your statements for the past seven years.
- Though you've never heard of something called the Alternative Minimum Tax, the very sound of that phrase is unsettling to you.
- You've had to hide under your bed to *avoid* getting a good job, with the American economy as strong as it has been.
- You've never heard of a politician in Washington trying to use federal tax policy to control your behavior in any way.
- The fifteenth day of April has always been just another spring day—unless you live in the Southern Hemisphere.

Doesn't sound like such a bad deal, does it? You've kept all the money you've earned. You've been getting five hundred bucks a month from the feds. And you've paid taxes only when you spent money.

Now that we've established your economic situation, along comes a politician who has a grand new scheme for a new tax system. Now, the true purpose of this politician's proposed new tax code is to take more of your power over your own economic life and transfer that power to Washington, D.C. The politician gets together with some D.C. power brokers and comes up with a grand idea. Before it can become the new law of the land, though, he has to explain it to you and get your support. After all, it's going to take a constitutional amendment to get this done.

Here's this caring, compassionate politician's great new idea—the one he claims will make your life so much more pleasant. First, the FairTax you've always lived with will be removed from the price of everything you buy. This will mean that everything will cost 23 percent less than it does now.

So far, so good. But put down the champagne, Charlie: it ain't what it seems.

The next step in this politician's grand plan is to have the federal government tax every single penny you earn. Now, you're a pretty successful kind of person, and this new tax plan is going to tax you based on how successful you are at making money. But hey! You might think it's perfectly fine for you to pay more taxes if you earn more money. After all, that's more or less the way it's been since you drew your first paycheck: the more you earned, the more you spent, and the more you spent, the more retail sales tax you ended up paying to the federal government.

Well, your politician friend has a bit of a twist for you.

Sure, you're going to pay more income tax as your income goes up. But here's the surprise: the more successful you are, the higher the income tax *rate* is going to be!

Oh! You want details? Well, for some reason this politician is a little reluctant to offer any specifics. But we've managed to look into a crystal ball and copy down the figures. As you absorb them, remember: up until now, all you've ever done is pay the federal government 23 cents of every dollar you spend. You've never paid anything on money you've invested or saved.

Under the grand new scheme, though, here's what you'd pay:[4]

- 10 percent of every dollar of your income less than $15,650
- 15 percent on every dollar of your income between $15,650 and $63,699
- 25 percent on every dollar of your income between $63,700 and $128,499
- 28 percent on every dollar of your income between $128,500 and $195,849
- 33 percent on every dollar of your income between $195,850 and $349,699
- 35 percent on every dollar of your income more than $349,700

---

4. These are 2007 tax schedule figures from the IRS for people who are married and filing jointly.

Let's assume you're in the middle-income bracket. How does this new plan sound? You used to pay a 23 percent inclusive sales tax on purchases past the poverty level; now you'll have to pay 25 percent—not just on what you spend but on what you earn! Push those earnings up a bit, and the rate climbs!

This character's really got your attention now, doesn't he?

What's more, not only will you be taxed, but so will every individual and every business that plays any role at all in bringing every single product you buy and every single service you use to the marketplace. Now, you can rest assured that these businesses and individuals aren't going to take these new federal taxes lying down. To them, the new federal taxes will be just another cost of doing business—and, like all other business expenses, they'll factor them into the cost of whatever they produce. These taxes will end up embedded in the prices of products in our retail marketplace. There goes that 23 percent break in retail prices you thought you were going to get.

Wait! There's more. Next, your political benefactor is going to take away your $500 per month sales tax rebate. Sure, you'll get some tax deductions under this plan—but those deductions won't come anywhere close to the prebate you've been receiving all your working life.

Finally, if you're not already dancing in the aisles over the prospect of this great new tax plan, there's one more detail he forgot to mention: a nifty little thing called payroll taxes!

All your life, Social Security and Medicare have been funded by the federal revenues generated by the FairTax. But the rates your politician is proposing for the new federal income tax won't cover the cost of Social Security and Medicare, so you're going to have to pay for them separately.

First let's take Social Security. Your employer is going to start deducting 6.2 percent from every one of your paychecks. It's going to be called a "contribution," but there will be nothing voluntary about it. Your employer will have to "match" that "contribution" with another 6.2 percent. Come on, now. You're smarter than that, aren't you? You realize that your employer is not going to merely swallow that 6.2 percent. Either it'll come out of your next pay raise (good luck on that for a while), or the price of whatever you're making and selling will have to go up. And of course, if you were to change jobs under this grand new plan, any new salary would be reduced by the employer's increased costs for this "matching contribution" nonsense.

Medicare? Nope, the income tax revenues won't cover that either. Just as you did with Social Security, you're going to get nailed with yet another new tax to cover Medicare! How much? Well, the new plan is going to use that same "matching contribution" idea, so you'll end up paying another 2.9 percent of everything you earn.

Are you adding all this up? You'll be paying 25 percent on your income for income taxes, plus those Social Security and Medicare taxes. So—including the matching—you're in the 40 percent range. And remember, right now you're paying only 23 percent on everything you spend above the poverty level.

Come on, folks, be serious. How in the world is any politician going to be able to sell such a ridiculous idea to you?

Wait! We're not through here. There are still more facets to this new tax system for you to consider:

- Do you have any investments? You've always been able to invest with absolutely no tax consequences. If this new tax idea becomes law, though, not only will you have to give the government a share of your earnings before you even invest them, but you'll also have to pay the government on any money you earn with that investment! It's going to be called a "capital gains" tax. What the government is really talking about is a tax on capitalism.
- We're going to have a death tax! Isn't that just grand? When you die, your family will have to file a complicated estate tax return. A huge amount of the wealth you've managed to build during your life will be sent to the government. Your survivors may well have to sell the family business in order to come up with the money to pay for these death taxes.

Oh, and just a few procedural details:

- You'll have to start keeping records of all of your financial transactions.

- Every year you'll have to spend thirty hours filling out your tax forms or hundreds of dollars to hire someone to fill them out for you.
- Trillions of dollars will leave the American economy to work in foreign markets, where the tax treatment will be much better. Billions more will be spent by businesses and individuals in this country to cover the cost of compliance with the new tax scheme.
- If you make mistakes on your federal tax forms, you'll be hit with a huge penalty and interest. You could even go to jail.
- The government will have access to all of your financial records to make sure you're paying what some politicians have decided is "your fair share."
- Politicians will soon learn they can curry favor with voters by pandering to their jealousies and raising taxes on the evil rich. If you work hard, that means you.
- Thousands of people will start earning big bucks inside the Beltway lobbying members of Congress for favorable tax treatment for their clients.
- America will no longer be the world's number one tax haven. Businesses will pack up and leave in search of a new home where they can do business without a tax component on capital and labor. One of the jobs lost could be yours.

But wait! you say. Why would any politician want to change the tax system this way? Why is he trying so hard—

spending so much money—to convince you that his new system will be so much better for you and the country than the simple national retail sales tax you've been paying your whole life?

One word: power.

The more politicians can control your access to your own wealth and earnings, the more powerful they are. The more politicians can affect businesses and important business decisions with tax policy, the more powerful they are. The more they can adversely affect the financial picture of one segment of our economy for the benefit of another, the more powerful they are. The more politicians can pander to the petty fears and jealousies of people by punishing high achievers for their efforts, the more powerful they are.

Under the FairTax, these politicians will have had no power to use tax policy to favor one group of voters over another for the benefit of votes. Bring in the new income tax scheme, and wonderful new horizons for manipulation and power brokering will open up for any politician who would like to use it. And what politician wouldn't?

There. With luck, this exercise has given you something of a new perspective on the FairTax and its benefits. Is it perfect? No. But on the other hand, think about what you've just read: if you lived under the FairTax now, would you be willing to switch back to our current system? If you really think you'd opt for this system after having lived under the FairTax virtually all your life, you might want to have your drinking water checked for hallucinogens.

Of course, after years of research, the development of a

133-page bill, and years of close examination and critique, we believe the FairTax should be passed as it is. At the same time, through the years we've heard some very interesting and valuable recommendations for improving it. For example, some people have suggested that the act could be made contingent on the repeal of the Sixteenth Amendment, the 1913 amendment that created the current system. Others have weighed the wisdom of adding a provision that a supermajority should be required to exempt or exclude any good or service. Neither of those provisions is in the bill as written, but they're worth some consideration.

Some have suggested that we have a lower rate on sales and a small tax on the incomes of very wealthy income earners. This is where we draw the line. Our current income tax began as a flat tax on high-income earners. It was flattened again in 1986. It has been amended 16,000 times in the last twenty years. Every nation that starts out with a little of each has wound up with a lot of both.

Our position is clear: one or the other—not both!

If we go back to the principles that the tax code must be simple, fair, voluntary, transparent, border neutral, and industry neutral as well as strengthen our retirement programs—and we manage to pass legislation that accomplishes those goals—we'll have succeeded.

Our vision for tomorrow is an America in which every American, including you, can be a voluntary taxpayer paying taxes when you choose, as much as you choose, according to how you choose to spend.

Our vision for tomorrow is an America where an individual driven to achieve and excel through hard work is not punished by a tax system that singles him out for mountains of record-keeping and paperwork, all leading to a punitive increase in his taxes.

Our vision for tomorrow is an America with a tax system that can be used to spread freedom across the world.

Under the FairTax Vision for Tomorrow, every time an American buys a loaf of bread or a new car, he'll know, to the penny, how much of that money is going to the federal government.

Our vision for tomorrow sees a government that's a partner with the business community and the people, not an adversary; a government with a tax system that encourages economic development and the creation of new business, rather than a government and a tax system that chase valued businesses to foreign shores.

Our vision for tomorrow is one where governance returns to the local level; where communities are allowed to make the important decisions regarding their government and their schools.[5] No longer will politicians be able to hide regulations and programs that control every aspect of our lives in 9 million words of confusing and draconian codes

---

5. Historians have said that it was the stated goal of our founders that in times of peace 95 percent of governance would come from the local level. It seems as if that situation has been reversed. Can you think of one thing that you are free to do with your life that does not have some element of federal control?

and regulations. The FairTax will demand political honesty. If Congress decides to come up with a new program or to expand a current program, that program will show up on the spending side of the ledger for you and other citizens to see. It's called transparency—and with the FairTax, with the beautiful simplicity of a tax system based on consumption spending, you'll be better equipped to hold your elected officials accountable for the decisions they make to expand the cost and scope of government.

Good for you? Sure. For the people wanting your votes? A little tougher for them.

Today, most Americans don't think twice about government spending. Why? Maybe because they've somehow convinced themselves that someone else is really paying for it. This is especially true for the bottom 50 percent of our income earners, who pay no income taxes and are disproportionately beneficiaries of government spending. It's also true for the vast majority of our retired citizens. Under the FairTax, nobody would pay federal taxes on the basic necessities of life. But when you make the choice to spend beyond those necessities, you will be taxed. Whether you are poor or retired, you will pay the tax on all spending above the poverty level. With more people actively participating in funding our government, more people will want to pay attention to just how that money is spent. As we said, good for you—but maybe not for the politicians.

Our vision for tomorrow sees an America where jobs are insourced, not outsourced. As you've seen, former secretary of the Treasury John Snow called it "the biggest magnet for capital and jobs in history." We will welcome legal immigrants to our country to do these jobs; not only will they contribute tax dollars to our government every time they buy a loaf of bread, but they'll have an incentive to come here legally and get in line to become citizens. Under the FairTax, you see, only legal residents will escape taxation on the cost of basic necessities. Prospective citizens will have a sense of ownership in the future of our country and will be just as interested as you are in throwing out the illegals who come here to take advantage of government-funded largesse or to get involved in criminal activity.

Our vision for tomorrow sees America becoming the safest and most secure tax haven for trillions of dollars currently languishing offshore. When these dollars return to our markets, your and your neighbors' nest eggs will grow dramatically. The capital infusion will create more jobs, and more consumption and revenues will help compensate for the growth of our entitlement programs. It will also reduce interest rates for all borrowers.

Our vision for tomorrow sees an America that will enjoy a virtual $400-billion-per-year tax cut. This is a good estimate of the amount of money that individuals and businesses now spend every year simply to figure out and obey our current tax code. With the tax code abolished and the collection process simplified, this money will stay in our pockets, where it can work for economic growth; it will no longer be spent to feed the federal bureaucracy.

Our vision for tomorrow sees America becoming an exporting powerhouse, selling goods and services into a global economy unburdened by the 22 percent tax component now burdening our price system. Our balances of trade and payments will improve because of it. Other nations' sales to Americans will face the same tax treatment as our sales to their citizens have faced for decades. Our imports will no longer have an advantage at the checkout counter over our domestically produced products.

Our vision for tomorrow sees an America where no one will be able to live under the radar. Beneficiaries of illicit money and illegal labor will pay their share of our government burden each time they buy a car or a loaf of bread.

Perhaps our most exciting vision for tomorrow is that our grandchildren will keep what they earn. They will not face a doubling of the payroll tax on every dollar they earn to pay for our retirement benefits. Their interest rates will be lower, making homes and cars more affordable. And their savings won't be penalized, so saving for *their* children's education, and for their own retirement, will be easier.

Are these grandiose ideas? Perhaps. But we don't consider them pipe dreams. We're confident that the economic revolution that would result from the FairTax, and the attendant transfer of power from the federal government to the people, would bring our vision for tomorrow to life. And we're not alone. Millions of Americans—from presidential candidates to renowned economists to union members—see the opportunities that await us as well.

Isn't this what life is all about? Don't we spend our lives trying to create a future for our children and grandchildren that's better than the world our parents left to us? We believe that our current tax code, which punishes initiative and thrift and rewards consumption, should be reversed, so that our children will have incentives to produce and invest and save—and thrive.

APPENDIX

THE PRESIDENT'S ADVISORY
PANEL ON TAX REFORM:
THE GOOD, THE BAD, AND THE UGLY

In telling the full story of the FairTax, we're sadly forced to include a group formally known as the President's Advisory Panel on Federal Tax Reform, which President Bush appointed early in 2005. We say "sadly" because an issue as large and complex as tax reform requires presidential leadership, and President Bush had a very real opportunity to be a leader on tax reform in 2004 and 2005. Instead of providing that leadership—and counter to the counsel of many members of Congress—the president appointed a panel to study the tax issue and make recommendations to him for reform.

For those of you who wonder exactly what the President's Advisory Panel is and what work it did, you're not alone—and that's a primary reason to consider the panel's effort a failure. In its final report, the panel stated that its goal was to "give voice to the frustrated American taxpayer and to provide a blueprint for lasting reform." That's an admirable goal that we all share, but by all accounts, not a single taxpayer found his or her voice in the report. Its recommendations didn't last past the news cycle of the day of its release. That is a complete failure by the panel's own yardstick—though, it must be said very loudly, blame for the failure rests not with the panel's members but with its structure and charge. Let's find out why.

The Panel's Structure and Charge

The tax panel was composed of some very bright minds on both the left and the right of the political and economic spectrum,[1] and it worked ferociously and collaboratively to produce its report on time and as instructed. But the panel was forced to work within some very specific constraints put upon it by President Bush, and it was those restraints—

---

1. In fairness, we're sure that our idea of "left" and "right" is very different from Nancy Pelosi's, Ted Kennedy's, or Hillary Clinton's. That said, the president deliberately appointed people with different views, and that breadth of views is apparent in both the panel's deliberations and its recommendations.

and the limitations of a committee structure in general—that doomed the effort.

Those of you who have served on panels or committees at your business, social club, neighborhood association, church, synagogue, or mosque know exactly what committees can do well and what they can't. Committees are very good at providing "consensus" solutions—strategies that blend together many divergent views and that everyone can tolerate. They're *not* good at providing leadership on controversial issues. It was no surprise, then, that the President's Advisory Panel was very successful at the former and a complete failure at the latter.

The panel's charge is often overlooked by those who comment on its work, but understanding the charge is critical to understanding the panel's report. The charge came in the form of Executive Order 13369, issued on January 7, 2005. In relevant part the order charged the panel as follows:

1. It was to produce a report—not for the president but for the secretary of the Treasury.
2. The report should be based on revenue-neutral tax policy.
3. The report should include options that
   a. Simplify the tax code to reduce administrative costs and burdens
   b. Share tax benefits and burdens in an appropriately progressive manner

   c. Recognize the importance of home ownership and charitable giving

   d. Promote economic growth and job creation

   e. Encourage work, saving, investment, and global competitiveness

4. The report should include at least one option that maintains the federal income tax.

5. The report was to be produced as soon as possible, but not later than July 31, 2005.[2]

If you were wondering why true tax reformers were opposed to the president creating this panel at the time, we think the language of that executive order makes it obvious. It's as if the president had been telling the panel and the nation:

> **Attention. Attention.** *My bold reform charge is to create a brand-new tax system for America . . . brand new except that it should keep progressive income tax system as its base . . . and it should keep current popular tax deductions . . . and it should keep the current distribution of tax benefits and burdens . . . and it should keep current levels of tax revenues . . . but other than that it should be newer, simpler, and better than what we have today.*

---

2. If you would like to read the Executive Order in its entirety, it can be found at www.whitehouse.gov/news/releases/2005/01/20050107-1.html.

The tax panel included some of the best minds in the business—but how much could it really do when "keep everything the way it is—but make it better" was its mandate? This is the definition of tinkering with the tax code, and it has no possibility of providing the fundamental economic restructuring that America needs, taxpayers want, and the FairTax hopes to provide.

You don't develop a plan for fundamental reform without carte blanche authority to tear up and throw away all that has come before.

Well, skipping forward eleven months and two president-mandated extensions to the report due date, we find that the panel members did absolutely everything they could to inject some creativity into their very narrow mandate. The panel offered not one but two tax reform proposals for the president—or rather the secretary of the Treasury—to consider. The report adhered to all of the president's restrictive guidelines, as well as the panel's self-imposed guideline of unanimity in its decisions and recommendations. Unfortunately, almost by definition, "unanimity" and "leadership" are opposites rather than synonyms.

Even so—even with the "keep everything the same" mandate and the decision to require unanimity of the diverse panel members—these consensus recommendations were attacked by every interest group benefiting from special tax preferences that would not have been renewed.[3]

_____

3. Make a note that even the relatively tame changes recommended by the tax panel drew immediate condemnation from the many in-

Further, as a consensus and compromise product, the panel's report had no primary sponsor to advocate for it. The panel's report was placed on a shelf at the Treasury Department and by all accounts has never been spoken of by the White House again.

The report was delivered in November 2005, and as we approach November 2007, we cannot find a single bill or proposal to come either out of the White House or from the Capitol that codifies these recommendations. To the panel that labored to fulfill President Bush's restrictive charge and sought to "give voice to the frustrated American taxpayer and to provide a blueprint for lasting reform," this silence represents both frustration and failure—and the panel members haven't been afraid to share their frustration and disappointment about it.

The Panel and FairTax

If the panel's report was shelved at the Treasury Department, why are we spending so much time on it here? The answer is that even though the panel's recommendations—

---

terests vested in the status quo. With the panel's minor changes—which got zero publicity—attracting the wrath of the vested interests, just try to imagine what is happening with the FairTax—which changes everything, has millions of supporters across the nation, and shows up in some media outlet almost every day of the week. You guessed it—we're not very popular with the special interests or the status quo crowd.

found in chapters 5, 6, and 7 of its report—haven't received much airplay (beyond a few swipes from grousing opponents), the commentary on a national retail sales tax found in its chapter 9 has found a welcoming audience in Fair-Tax opponents. Even though the chapter dealt primarily with traditional sales taxes and largely avoided the FairTax, our opponents still love to say, "But the president's tax panel said [insert your favorite rehashed criticism here] about the FairTax." To avoid any confusion, then, we wanted to devote a moment's attention to the report's ninth chapter.

To our reading, the panel's chapter 9 seems out of place. Coming as the final chapter in a long report of rigorous comparisons and economic insights, chapter 9 is devoid of both. In their place, we find political commentary and a string of statements of the obvious. It's as though the panel simply ran out of steam before it reached chapter 9 but felt compelled to cobble together a list of reasons why it did not choose to recommend a true consumption tax such as a sales tax. And compelled it was, since throughout its eleven-month process the panel was inundated with words, letters, and e-mails from FairTax supporters and volunteers. As far as we can tell, the FairTax dominated the public's comments to the panel.

Though it's a moot point now, that public support is still on the public record: you can find it at the tax panel's Web site, www.taxreformpanel.gov, in the public comment section. In fact, all the tax panel information is posted on the Web site, so if you read something here

that you'd like to explore further, that site is a good re-
source for everything that happened between the executive order in January 2005 and the final report that
November.

Tax Panel Basics: Solid

For all of you whose heart rates peaked while reading our
book, we recommend the tax panel report to you. In parts,
it really is a page-turner. If you do read it, we think you'll
find what we found: it begins strong, with a host of insights
about reform, but finishes weak, with a series of cursory
overviews and dismissals of alternatives to the panel's proposals. We'll get to the negatives later, though. First let's
review the positives.

Chapter 1 makes a powerful case for reform, citing
many of the facts and statistics you've heard us use. The
panel talks about complexity, noting that Americans pay
an extra billion dollars in taxes every year simply because
they do not itemize and that 60 percent of Americans must
now pay a professional to do their taxes. It talks about compliance costs, noting what the amount of money that
Americans spend filling out their tax forms would fund,
and we quote, "the Department of Homeland Security, the
Department of State, NASA, the Department of Housing
and Urban Development, the Environmental Protection
Agency, the Department of Transportation, the United
States Congress, our federal courts, and all of the federal

government's foreign aid."[4] We call that big and wasted money.

The panel points out that the epidemic of noncompliance created by the current code costs each honest taxpayer an extra two thousand dollars a year in additional taxes. It looks at the arbitrariness of the code, noting that increasing your income by 50 percent can increase your tax burden by 140 percent. Chapter 1 offers charts to show that marginal income tax rates in the current code can rise to more than 30 percent for a family with an income of just $30,000 a year. That's 30 percent *in addition to* the 15 percent payroll tax burden, mind you. A 45 percent marginal rate on a $30,000 annual income is what is happening today—and that's coming straight from the tax panel report. Tell us again why working America should prefer the current system to the 23 percent FairTax!

Chapter 2 offers a thorough history of the income tax code. From a picture of one of the very first tax forms to a chart depicting the more than sixteen thousand changes to the income tax code since 1986, the panel covers the topic well. Though these early chapters of the panel's report are very good, it must be noted that there is not a single reference in these pages to the payroll tax—the largest tax most Americans pay and a tax that collects almost as much (and occasionally more) from working Americans than the per-

---

4. Report of the President's Advisory Panel on Federal Tax Reform, *Simple, Fair, and Pro-Growth: Proposals to Fix America's Tax System,* November 2005, p. 2.

sonal income tax does. We understand that the panel considered it outside of its charge, but with more than 80 percent of Americans losing more of their paycheck to it than the income tax, it seems foolhardy at best to discuss tax reform without addressing the payroll tax. Yet that's exactly what the panel members thought the president had instructed them to do. We're not blaming the panel for this gross failure, but it sure would have made its work more useful if its members had bucked their restrictive mandate and included this vital element. Thank goodness the FairTax does just that.

Chapter 3 does a good job of explaining tax basics—things like the different tax bases and the definition of tax incidence. Chapters 4, 5, 6, and 7 discuss the two reform models that the tax panel proposed and how it arrived at them. We won't go into detail on those here, because, as we said, (a) they were apparently forgotten by the administration as soon as they were proposed and (b) while the panel did the best it could within the very limited "status quo" latitude the president gave it, its two proposals didn't come anywhere close to the breadth of reform we FairTax supporters are demanding. (If you want to read the panel's proposals, any of the chapters we've discussed, or simply the tax panel's report in its entirety, you can find it chapter by chapter on the Tax Panel Web site [www.taxreformpanel .gov] or you can download the whole thing from the Government Printing Office.[5])

---

5. The direct link to the report on the GPO Web site is http:// permanent.access.gpo.gov/lps64969/taxreformwholedoc.pdf.

Don't think our describing the tax panel recommendations generously as "tinkering" and "status quo" is just sour grapes because we didn't get our way. Our view was echoed by commentators like Robert Novak in the *Chicago Sun-Times:* "10 months, and tax panel has zero to show." Then–House Majority Leader Tom DeLay described the recommendations as "too small, and at bottom they only simplify and slightly improve a broken system." *Investment News* agreed: "Tax Reform Plans Seen as Too Tame."

If you need a good laugh, though, you should take a look at a few of the headlines that appeared after the panel's report was released. From the sounds of its opponents— those with a vested interest in the current system who opposed even the relatively minor changes proposed by the panel—the sky was falling and all was nearly lost. From California Treasurer Phil Angelides: "The Tax Plan that Cheats California." From the National Association of Realtors: "All homeowners will suffer if this policy is enacted." From now–House Speaker Nancy Pelosi: "The president's tax panel would demolish the building blocks middle-class Americans use to reach the American dream." From a newswire: "Life [Insurance] Agents Group Warns That Tax Changes Could Spell Doom for Industry." All this commotion over proposals that we and others call "minor"! Remember this as you read any criticisms of the FairTax. If the special interests use words like "cheat," "suffer, "demolish," and "doom" to describe the tax panel's report, you better put on a seat belt before reading their comments about the FairTax.

Tax Panel Report: Nuggets of Wisdom

Before we get to some of the lunacy (or maybe "hatchet job" is a better term) in the final chapter of the tax panel's report, let's quickly go through some of the important lessons to be drawn from the tax panel's experience and some of the panel's insights that demonstrate just how important it is that we make the FairTax a reality.

Lesson 1: Balancing everyone's concerns is difficult if not impossible. You simply have to prioritize your goals and then sell the result. The tax panel brought together people from across the economic and political spectrum and then adopted unanimity as a leadership model. That approach not only failed to make the people on the far left and far right happy, but it also failed to please or excite the middle. If tax reform were easy, it would have been done already.

Lesson 2: You can expect to take fire from everyone who favors the status quo. As we saw above, even a relatively simple consensus proposal like that of the tax panel was smeared by everyone who preferred the status quo. William Gale of the Brookings Institution (who rarely has supportive words for the FairTax but whose criticisms have often helped improve the FairTax) responded to the panel's special-interest critics perfectly: "These are substantial, significant, well-founded ideas that need to be taken together as a package. . . . [The panelists] did what they were supposed to do, and they did a very good job. Everyone wants their own subsidies first, and then they'll take simplification."[6] One of the things we find most rewarding about working with FairTax volunteers is that rarely does anyone ask "What's in it for me?" Instead, the prevailing sentiment is "If it's good for America, I'm in."

Lesson 3: Tax reform is complicated and won't sell itself. It needs an advocate. No one fought for the tax panel's proposals, many people fought against them, and they died a quiet death. Tax reform needs an advocate—a presidential advocate—and it needs millions of grassroots supporters.

America needs tax reform, and the FairTax is closer than any other proposal or idea that we know of to amassing the advocates necessary to make it happen.

Crazy Chapter 9: The Tax Panel Hit Job on the Sales Tax

It's in chapter 9 of its report that the panel addresses the question of why it failed to recommend a national retail sales tax. Keep in mind that the panel mentions the FairTax only three times in the entire report; chapter 9 is hardly an attack on the FairTax. On the contrary, it's an effort to discredit the general idea of a national sales tax. Why the panel chose to pursue that course is still a mystery to us, but the biased conclusions in its final chapter are a strange contrast to the good work in the rest of the report.

---

6. Pamela Yip, "Tax Panel Proposals Criticized." *The Dallas Morning News,* November 2, 2005.

Chapter 9 opens by stating that the panel rejected the idea of a sales tax for two specific reasons. First, it charged, replacing the income tax with a sales tax that doesn't have a prebate (as the FairTax does, of course) would shift the tax burden more toward middle- and lower-income Americans and thus would not be "appropriately progressive" as mandated by the president. Second, including a prebate (like the one in the FairTax) would, they claimed, "inappropriately increase the size and scope of government." Let that settle in for a moment.

The first objection—that a sales tax without a prebate is unfair to lower-income Americans—recurs throughout chapter 9. We probably agree with that sentiment, but we don't know of anyone anywhere in the nation who is proposing such a thing. Congratulations to the tax panel for taking a strong stand against something absolutely no one supports!

The second objection is the first of a string of flat out odd statements that seem to be thrown into chapter 9 that claim that abolishing the income tax would "inappropriately increase the size and scope of government." How strange that the panel tasked with reforming the income tax—that most intrusive, powerful, and despised of all American institutions—chose to preserve the income tax because the proposal supported by Boortz (the Libertarian) and Linder (the conservative) would be too much big government. This was flabbergasting: neither of us can remember ever being accused of supporting big government, period. If the thought wasn't so crazy, it would have hurt our feelings.

Now, as we've said, the prebate is the toughest part of

the FairTax to get your mind and emotions around, and we're constantly looking for ways to improve it. Our beef with the tax panel isn't that the prebate isn't a cause for concern. Our beef with the tax panel is that the prebate isn't a reason to give up on tax reform altogether. It just seems like an excuse for the panel to say no.

Still think we're paranoid? Here's another odd note. As you know, the FairTax is premised on an extremely large tax base. This is part of its fundamental intent: the larger the base, the lower the rate can be, and the lower the rate, the less intrusive the tax will be on a citizen's decision making. In chapter 3, the tax panel does a good job of explaining why large tax bases are good and small tax bases are bad. Yet in chapter 9, after noting the large base of the FairTax, the panel goes on to explain why that base might shrink over time due to legislative changes.

Hmmm . . . "Beware of the FairTax—it might be changed in the future."

On what level does this make sense? There's no warning elsewhere in the report that either of the tax panel's proposals will be just as vulnerable to change by a future Congress. There's no warning that a VAT could be changed by a future Congress. But a number of pages in chapter 9 sound the ominous warning that someday someone might change the rules of a national sales tax. Can't we just agree that all taxes are subject to change and the voter must stand up and say "Yea" or "Nay"? That's an American Government 101 lesson that belonged in chapter 1, 2, or 3 of the panel's history section—not a complaint to be held in reserve until it could be aimed at sales taxes in particular.

The strangely cobbled together pages of chapter 9 also include this shocking revelation: "Moreover, unless the states repealed their existing sales taxes, most consumers would pay both federal and state sales tax on many goods." Shocking, isn't it? Well, in case you weren't shocked, the tax panel threw in a big number to tell you how much that combined state and federal sales tax might be.

The FairTax rate is a big number . . . and when you combine it with state sales tax rates, the number gets even bigger. But it's important to remember two things: first, it's exactly what we're all collectively paying today; second, the very same big, scary math applies to the income tax, in which states collect additional income tax on top of what we pay the feds.

Did you catch the section of the report that clarifies that you'll need to pay state income taxes on top of the income taxes it proposes? No, probably not—because it isn't there. Did you catch the spot where it highlights the really big rate number that represents the combined federal and state income tax rates you'd pay under the panel's proposals? Nope, not there either. And frankly, we don't think it should be. We're talking about federal taxes, and of course the state tax situation will still exist in addition. We just can't figure out why the panel felt the need to bring them up at all—and then only in the context of the sales tax.

Still think we're crazy? We have dozens more examples, but we'll just include one more. On page 220 of the report, you'll find a section concerning state sales taxes. It's unlikely that states would model their sales tax on the federal sales tax, the report says, because states would fail to follow the federal model, and confusion and pandemonium would ensue. Thus sayeth page 220.

Now turn to page 221. Here you'll find a section talking about state income taxes. The panel worries about removing the federal income tax because most states have modeled their income tax on it. Because states could no longer use the federal model, confusion and pandemonium would ensue. Thus sayeth page 221.

We're certain that there's a grain of truth on both pages, but can the tax panel really fault the national sales tax for both? If states love following a federal model (as page 221 suggests), they'll be pleased to have the federal sales tax to follow. If states hate following a federal model (as page 220 suggests), they'll be pleased to be rid of the federal income tax so that they can do their own thing. We don't claim to know which one is true, but isn't it a little strange for the tax panel to use both of these two concerns—complete opposites—as reasons to oppose a federal sales tax? And, yes, you guessed it, none of the other chapters says a word about the angst that the tax panel's own proposals might cause the states that have come to rely on the federal model. Nor is there any discussion of the money that states lose annually in sales taxes and how many are requesting a federal system for coordinating catalog and Internet sales. Shocking, these omissions.

So when you read chapter 9 of the panel's report—or,

more important, when you hear someone citing the tax panel to attack the FairTax—keep all this in mind. We don't know why this chapter is so bizarre. But we think you see what we mean.

Oh, you remember that we said the FairTax got three mentions in the panel's report? The first was the reference to its large base; the second was for the prebate system. The third was in a little box on page 217 of the report—a note suggesting that FairTax tax rate is wrong.

How did the panel come to that conclusion? Well, we've asked that question. But the tax panel *declined* to share its math with us—and our request for backup through the Freedom of Information Act is still working its way through the process. But we're not worried. As you might imagine, when the FairTax was first created, we had no idea what the rate should be. The good folks at Americans for Fair Taxation had to hire some of the top economic minds in the country to tell us the proper rate. The AFFT received three calculations of the rate from three leading national economists, and we're rather comforted by the fact that one of those three economists was none other than tax panel member Dr. James Poterba.

The rate he recommended? 23.1 percent.

We don't need to quibble about that 0.1 percent, do we?

ACKNOWLEDGMENTS

We would first like to thank our wives for all of the support that they have given to us during the writing process. Having been through this process with us once already, they knew exactly what to expect . . . and they were 100 percent behind us anyway. Having them share our dream for a FairTax world has meant the world to us.

We want to acknowledge all of the professionals at FairTax.org who have supported us with their time, comments and passion throughout this process. In particular, we want to acknowledge Karen Walby—AFFT Director of Research—both for her contribution of time and intellect to this book and for her efforts promoting the FairTax effort in general. We also want to thank Ken Hoagland—AFFT Communications Director—and Dennis Calabrese—AFFT Director of Strategy and Planning—for their help with the book as well as their never-ending passion for bringing the

FairTax to fruition, passion that reveals itself in myriad ways daily.

We must again acknowledge the work of the Tax Foundation, a nonpartisan tax research group. Celebrating its 70th year in 2007, the Tax Foundation is a tireless examiner of the American tax code and its effect on American taxpayers. You will have seen several references to this group's fine work in the previous pages, and you can find much more at www.taxfoundation.org.

Finally, and most importantly, we want to acknowledge the hundreds of thousands of volunteers behind the FairTax movement. Without them, the FairTax would simply be a collection of clever thoughts on paper at the Library of Congress. With them, the FairTax is a great hope for the future of the American economy. We try to acknowledge and thank these volunteers at every opportunity, but no amount of recognition can convey our admiration for these carpenters, doctors, miners, nurses, teachers, policemen, truck drivers, accountants, bankers, firefighters, small business owners, and more who give of themselves to make the FairTax a reality for their children and grandchildren. You see them at political rallies and think-tank gatherings; you read and hear their words in opinion columns and call-in shows; and you see their passion displayed through t-shirts, bumper stickers, and lapel pins. Even more frequently, however, you see them as a thoughtful coworker at the water cooler, a committed cousin at a family gathering, or an enthusiastic parent next to you at the PTA or your child's Little League game. We still live in a time where the people can rule their government, but it cannot be done without the interest and commitment of millions. To all of you who have invested yourself in the FairTax, we acknowledge you and thank you. With the support of Americans like you, America will have the FairTax.